SOUL WEAVING

How to Shape your Destiny and Inspire your Dreams

Betty K. Staley

Hawthorn Press

Published by Hawthorn Press, Hawthorn House, 1 Lansdown Lane, Stroud, Gloucestershire, GL5 1BJ, UK
Tel: (01453) 757040 Fax: (01453) 751138

Cover design by Ivon Oates
Typesetting by Hawthorn Press
Printed in the UK by Redwood Books, Wiltshire

British Library Cataloguing in Publication Data applied for

ISBN 1 869 890 05 1

Contents

Section II: the Seven Soul Qualities and the Journey through Life

SECTION III:
TWELVE WINDOWS INTO THE WORLD

SECTION IV: SELF DEVELOPMENT:
STRIVING FOR WHOLENESS

DEDICATION:
To Jim, for your love, support, and patience.

Introduction

At the end of the 20th century, people feel an urgency to understand themselves, to relate their inner life to their outer life. They may dwell on their more instinctive experiences or on their higher ideals. They may buy self–help books or confessional autobiographies, watch 'tell–all' programs, attend workshops, or join groups with those who have had similar experiences, to aid in their attempts to overcome weaknesses, or to gain strength through mutual support.

On radio and television programs and in books, people share their deepest, darkest secrets. Sensationalist confessions of sexual perversions, abuse, violence, and satanic rituals are revealed in front of thousands of viewers, listeners, and readers.

At the same time, in other programs and books, people are describing spiritual experiences. Previously, if people revealed experiences with spiritual beings or described near-death experiences in a public forum, they were laughed at or even considered mentally unstable. The only people to take such conversation seriously were religious leaders. However, accounts of near-death experiences, meetings with angels, or encounters with a being of light who brings comfort during a time of despair bear so many common elements that they are now taken increasingly seriously.

People are changing. In our time, there is a deep desire to penetrate such subjects as the nature of the human being and our relationship to seen and unseen worlds. This interest is shared by people all over the world, and is enhanced by global communication such as the Internet.

In addition to a desire to understand spiritual experiences, there is a recognition that we can understand our behavior and transform it to something higher. The human biography has been recognized as the drama in which we act out our highest as well as our lowest intentions. In addition to enthusiasm for exploring outer space with rockets and satellites, we see intense interest in exploring *inner* space – the place of the soul.

It has been common for hundreds of years to regard the human being as a duality – as body and mind, or body and soul, or body and spirit. This view, separating the human being into two parts which seemed disconnected from each other, has long been reflected in everyday life, for example in an outer life which includes job and family responsibilities for most of the week, and an inner life focused mainly on weekly attendance at church or temple. Rudolf Steiner, Austrian philosopher, spiritual researcher and educator (1861– 1925), drew attention to a threefold human nature which would replace such duality with a more holistic image, enabling us better to understand the interconnectedness of man's inner and outer nature.

According to this view, the human constitution includes body, soul *and* spirit. The physical body includes those characteristics which depend on heredity, such as sex, race, height, bone structure, coloring, features, and even predisposition to certain illnesses.

The spirit is that part of us which is eternal. We connect with our spiritual selves when we illumine our thoughts with ideals such as truth or goodness, when we contemplate God, when we listen to our consciences, and when we glimpse the higher nature of another human being. We work on our spirit through prayer, meditation, and devotion.

Between the physical body and the spirit is the world of the soul. The soul includes everything that we experience in our actions, our emotions, and in our thoughts – in willing, feeling, and thinking. Desires, such as hunger, thirst, and sex, arise in our physical bodies and demand to be satisfied. Ideals, spiritual values, and truths shine in on these desires and create a tension. The soul is the meeting ground where our 'I' weaves these elements together. Do we give in to every whim enticing us, or do we set goals to accomplish our hopes and dreams? How do we live our lives? How do we transform our 'lower' selves so that we develop healthier, more integrated lives in which body, soul, and spirit are in balance? How do we become our true selves?

The 'I' is the 'higher self, the ego, pure spirit. The physical body is like a house in which our 'I' lives. The 'I' is the center of soul-life. It works through our thinking, our feeling, and our deeds to transform them. The 'I' works through thinking so that we are able to connect with the spirit, through feeling so we can become conscious of ourselves as individuals, and in our actions – the fruits of our will – to express itself in each particular stage of development. The 'I' lives in the house of the human being, forming, shaping, and creating. The manifestation of the 'I' in our soul life is our personality.

All our lives we express ourselves through thinking, feeling, and willing, but *one* of these soul forces predominates at each stage of life. For example, willing or action is strongest during early childhood. The child generally acts without conscious thought or feeling. What the child sees someone else do, she[1] must do also. Through imitation, children learn to walk and speak. Imitation is also at work in their absorbing of language.

For older children, however – between ages seven to fourteen – the feeling life is the dominant aspect of soul development. When a child feels joy or sadness, excitement or stillness, wonder or terror, her relationship to the world is stimulated. Therefore, stories are the most effective means of strengthening the emotional or feeling life of the soul, and that is why the choice of stories (or content of films and television shows) has such a strong impact on a child's moral development. Violence or compassion have very different impacts on children's feeling life. A strong feeling life helps develop the inner world of imagination. The strength of feelings during this period continues to affect the soul life of the young person as she grows into adulthood.

From ages fourteen to twenty-one, thinking is the main soul-force being developed. Through thinking, the adolescent learns to discipline the will and bring objectivity to feelings. Through the development of thinking, a young person gains access to universal laws. An active life of healthy movement and will in a child's early years and the strong experience of moral stories and imagination in the middle years serve as a powerful foundation for the development of thinking in the adolescent years.

The experiences of will, feeling, and thinking during the first twenty-one years of life are the seeds for what will develop in later years.

	Thinking
SOUL FORCES —	Feeling
	Willing

In this book, I describe three of the aspects of our soul life – temperament, soul quality, and archetype. Each is most strongly connected with one of the soul forces, although the other two are always involved as well.

Willing – Temperament

We could say that the temperament is that part of the soul most strongly connected to the physical body, to the will. Just as our will is unconscious, so too is the temperament. It is as embedded in our psyche as are our habits – and is just as difficult to change. The temperament reveals itself usually around age five and continues to express itself through childhood until puberty. Parents and teachers can work with the temperament during childhood. The temperament continues to influence us from puberty on, but often differently than in the earlier years. Our 'I' can work to transform it. For example, we can do exercises to help us develop the positive, selfless aspects of our temperaments.

Feelings – Soul Quality

The soul quality has to do with the habits of our feelings, with our attitudes and gestures. We say that people have 'habits of mind'. They also have habits of feeling. These habits or patterns express our emotional relationship to the people we meet, to our situations, to our work, and we call this a person's 'soul quality'. The soul quality reveals itself in adolescence when it interacts with the temperament from earlier years. Developing an understanding of the seven soul qualities allows us to work with them as an actor might with character types.

Thinking – Archetype

The archetype offers us at least twelve ways of viewing the world. It has to do with the habits of our thinking, with the thought of who we are in the world. Archetypes are universal and appear in fairy tales, myths, and legends around the world. Behind the personality stands the archetype, the idea, of each particular human being. How we realize this idea has much to do with how we consciously address the archetypes that reveal themselves in us. Our 'I' can work to bring out the highest aspect of the archetype so that we are able to realize ourselves in our highest ideals.

Together, temperament, soul quality, and archetype are the elements with which I weave my life.

In *Tapestries: Weaving Life's Journey,*[2] I focused on the structure of the relationships we form throughout our lives. I chose the tapestry as an image of the human biography because of the weaving elements it incorporates. In a person's life, the warp, which the weaver carefully threads onto the loom before the weaving can begin, consists of those elements which were established before birth – our gender, family, birth order, and nationality.

Who weaves this tapestry? It is the 'I,' the spiritual part of our being, transcending heredity and shaping us, weaving a weft of spiritual and earthly influences, learning from experiences, passing through stages of development, leading us into destiny meetings, whispering to us in our dreams, and inspiring us.

Now, in *Soul Weaving,* we will go on to look at these further aspects that contribute to our personalities – temperaments, soul qualities, and archetypes – and our relationship to spiritual development. Our personalities are very complex. Each of us has a unique design that represents our life. The physical body serves as the tapestry's warp. Our temperaments give us the texture of the design. The soul quality gives the color. Our 'I' is the Soul Weaver. For the rest of our lives, our 'I' works in relationship to our physical body; it works to transform and harmonize our temperaments and our soul qualities, and it works to bring our life's goals to fruition, aspiring ultimately to fulfil the perfection of our archetypes.

Design has always fascinated me. A simple turn of a kaleidoscope changes myriad crystal forms into newly arranged patterns of color; a surging wave retreats and leaves behind new patterns on the damp sand; the sun creates patterns of shade and light on the leaves of trees; the decision to turn right instead of left changes the design of a day (or a life). Design is the expression of pattern and form in life.

It is only in the final sounding of our years that we can see what the overall pattern – the soul weaving of our lives – has become. At any point along the way we can stop, retreat, observe, reflect on, and contemplate the pattern up to that point. We can decide to continue the design of the tapestry. Design in nature, design in human life, and design in art are all expressions of the same magnificent spiritual forces that work from beyond the physical world, transforming earthly substance and human experience into something majestic.

For the last thirty years, I have been a teacher, mainly of adolescents but also of younger children and adults. Throughout these years, the thread guiding me has been my interest in the human being. As a college student majoring in psychology in the late 1950s, I found the opportunities for graduate study very limited in scope. Most psychologists were either Freudians or Behaviorists, and a few were involved in parapsychology. When I was introduced to the works of Rudolf Steiner, I found a perspective on human life that intrigued me and which continues to do so today. I moved to England to study Waldorf education, to learn more about Steiner's anthroposophy and to travel in Europe.

As I journeyed across the Atlantic by ship, I met a man who was going to Switzerland to study Carl Jung's work. This was my introduction to Jung; I began reading his works, and I have been interested in them ever since, especially his insights into the language of the unconscious and mythology. I have never had Jungian training, but I was privileged for about five years to be part of a study group, composed mainly of Jungians, who studied the literature of Dante, Dostoyevsky, Shakespeare and others. We all brought insights from our various points of view and I learned a great deal from the Jungians.

Introduction

During my Waldorf teacher training, I chose Freud, Jung, and Steiner as my thesis subject. I was little aware at the time that this theme, emerging when I was twenty–one, would set a pattern for my thinking for years to come.

Several times during my life, I have come to crossroads where I considered resuming graduate study for a career in psychology. Each time, my depth of commitment to teaching and especially to Waldorf education has brought me back to my main life's work. However, my interest in psychology – in the human being – has never diminished and has remained an underlying thread in my teaching and in my work with adolescents.

Another thread has been my love of crafts, especially knitting, sewing, weaving, quilting, and architectural design. The more I worked with design, the more I realized that it was a common element in the two aspects of my life that I loved so deeply. Whether designing school activities – planning curriculum, arranging schedules, studying history, geography, or literature, exploring child development – or designing a craft project such as a quilt or a sweater, or working out how to reconfigure the space in our house, I found that I was working with the same process: bringing together elements of design.

It's not surprising therefore, that, in trying to understand the complexity of the human being, I have found the metaphor of design to be helpful. Elements of personality such as temperaments, soul attitudes, and archetypes, contribute significantly to the design of each human journey. Each element is part of the pattern, contributing to a larger design. By looking at the whole pattern, however, we can gain a picture of the Soul Weaving that has gone on.

Note on Gender & Pronouns

As in my earlier books, I have chosen to alternate the use of masculine and feminine pronouns in cases of indefinite gender. This is to avoid the continual use of a masculine pronoun (unless a feminine pronoun is clearly indicated). While wishing to honor today's heightened consciousness of the impact of gender-words, I also want to avoid the awkward 'he/she' contortions of those who seek to write grammatically without offending feminist sensibilities. In this book, therefore, in cases where gender is indefinite, I have used feminine forms in the odd-numbered chapters and masculine in the even-numbered.

Section I

Transforming the Temperaments in Adult Life: Facing Our Gifts and Challenges

The temperaments

When the child is born, we are filled with wonder at the perfection of the physical body. Each birth is a miracle. Each child is unique. In addition to our uniqueness, though, there are common patterns of behavior that we follow. In the first five or six years the energy of the child is directed to the growing physical body. All children follow general laws of growth. At first infants cannot hold up their head. Then they are able to do so and look around them. Gradually they are able to sit, crawl, and stand. Each new step is welcomed with a special joy as steps to further independence. The main activity during these early years has to do with the growth and maturing of the physical body.

Around six or seven the stage of physical growth reaches a plateau. The child loses some of her baby teeth. This is a sign that something basic is changing (just as menstruation is a sign of physical and emtional change in puberty). A new capacity is being born. The formative forces of the life organism (or etheric body, as Steiner calls it) have completed their first great task and are now freed for new tasks. With the 'birth' or release of the etheric body, the energy available as a result can be used for thinking. Before this time, emphasis on memory or 'learning' takes away energy from the primary task of growth. Because the etheric or life body is now freed from the task of supporting growth, a new aspect of the child's being is awakened. This is the temperament – which arises out of the interaction of physical and etheric bodies.

As the ancients did, Rudolf Steiner identified four temperaments – choleric, phlegmatic, sanguine, and melancholic. Each is related to a particular aspect of the physical body. The phlegmatic temperament tends to be connected with a heavy body, with the fluids in the body. A phlegmatic child feels this heaviness and is prone to move slowly. One can liken the phlegmatic temperament to a quiet pond (Still water runs deep!) or to the rhythmic tide of the ocean. Except for the occasional storm, one can rely on the phlegmatic taking things in her stride, approaching life methodically, disliking being rushed, exerting a calm mood over a group, and finding satisfaction in the status quo.

The melancholic temperament tends to feel burdened by the body. Often the child walks with head bent over a bit. It is as if the earth were pulling and weighing her down with worries and troubles. The melancholic child is closely connected with her body, is sensitive to *how fabrics feel – whether they are scratchy or smooth. She is sensitive to the texture of food. Some may feel the melancholic is supersensitive, even fussy, but she can't help it because she is so connected with the way her physical body feels. It is not surprising that melancholic children tend to have recurring headaches and stomach aches.*

A sanguine child is light as air, resembling a butterfly flitting from flower to flower. This child is hardly in his body, but instead expands into the atmosphere around him. He walks with a light step, responding to the warmth of feelings around him rather than the feeling of the earth itself. He is centered in his nervous system, his eyes dart here, there, and everywhere. He is easily distracted and finds it hard to remember where things are.

The choleric child is fully centered in her body, solidly anchored in her muscles. She walks with a sturdy step, ready for action at any moment. Like a flame, she is hot – ready to explode, quick to take control of a group, convinced she is the only one to make things happen. She is first, strongest, and best. She can count on her body to serve her for any task she takes on.

All children have the possibility of expressing all four temperaments, but one is usually dominant. As children come into puberty, the soul qualities begin to emerge, and the temperament then recedes into the background.

Chapter 1.
The Temperaments and
the Life Phases

Imagine the following: You have before you four jars of paint – red, yellow, blue, and green – several brushes, and a stack of painting paper. I mention the name of someone we all know, a person with a bold, aggressive way of speaking and acting, and I ask you to paint, using all four colors to express the way she behaves. You may use one color or any combination of colors. When we have finished, I think most of us would find that we have used a strong red somewhere on the page. When I mention another person, known for her gentleness, however, we may let blue dominate the page. We will probably use the other colors in slightly different proportions, depending very much on how well we know the person and how often we are able to see what else expresses itself through her.

The next day we do this exercise again. We find that our paintings are slightly different. And on the third day as well. The relationships between the four colors are constantly in flux, but a dominating color theme persists from day to day. So it is with each of us. Our thoughts, feelings, ideals, jealousies, our general approach to life and to our fellow human beings, as well as the way we feel about ourselves, may be dynamically expressed through colors. These are not so much physical as soul colors. What we have been trying to express by our choice of colors is what we know as the temperaments.

Each of us has our own way of meeting other people. For example, the door opens. One person is curious who it might be while another is annoyed and does not want to be bothered. Yet another couldn't care less who comes, while a fourth is ready to ward off some sort of threat or imposition. These are all expressions of what lives within our temperaments.

Temperaments were first described by Hippocrates and later by the Greek physician Galen in the second century A.D. Temperament, from the Latin verb *temperare,* means 'to mix, to combine, to blend' and has to do with mixing and balancing of the bodily fluids and their effect on the soul. The idea that the physical body could have an influence on the soul was generally accepted with some modifications until the 19th century. An exception was the Enlightenment view, typified by John Locke, who described the individual as a blank slate, ready to be filled by sense impressions coming from the environment. According to Locke and other Enlightenment thinkers, bodily constitution had no influence on the soul. After about 1900, the so-called 'Nature/Nurture Controversy' was in full swing with 'nurture' seen as the dominant influence from 1900 to the 1970s. Examples of this view include the work of the behaviorists, such as Ivan Pavlov and B. F. Skinner. The psychoanalytic theory of Sigmund Freud considered that children were all born equal. The reason they behave so differently, the Freudians said, had to do with the way their parents treated them. With such a strong emphasis on what was influencing the child from outside, temperaments had no place in modern psychological theory. Interest in temperaments also waned in American psychological circles partly because of concern that any view which claimed that behavior was influenced by physiology would lend itself to assertions of superiority or inferiority about one or more of America's immigrant communities. To counter this concern, the view was put forward that all children were similar at birth, and it was only opportunity which resulted in people developing different behaviors.

In the 1970s, however, a group of psychological researchers became interested in the question of temperaments. In studying infants they noted different behavioral qualities which they attributed to biological and neurological influences. As researchers began to study animals and humans, raised in the same (or as similar as possible) surroundings, they saw significantly different behavior patterns, and began to question the origin of these patterns. They looked to inherited physiological differences that showed themselves in temperament behavior.

Harvard psychology professor Jerome Kagan writes:

Research on human temperament has until now been peripheral ... because the phenomena of temperament are not amenable to experiments and involve differences among people, not universal qualities. But I suspect that this position will change in the future, for psychology has remained close to study of the brain. Neuroscience is a biological discipline and biology is the science of exceptions. Each species differs from the next in small details of physiology, anatomy, and behavior. That fact will motivate psychologists interested in human behavior to recognize that, on many occasions, they should expect that only some individuals will react to an event in a particular way and that uniform consequences will not always occur. The acceptance of that principle will force confrontation with the question *why*. When that time comes, the study of temperaments may become a major focus of psychological inquiry, as it was in Classical Greece and Rome and during the Middle Ages and Renaissance. Signs of this change emerged in the 1960s. [1]

When he developed Waldorf education in 1919, Rudolf Steiner spoke about temperaments. He described how teachers who understood the temperaments could develop a heightened sensitivity to children's behavior, and recognize that particular behavior may not be a result of obstinacy or external influence but the product of physiological-psychological causes. Steiner also stressed that each person is influenced by all four temperaments, and that the dominant temperament should be seen as a *tendency toward* certain behavior rather than as its determinant. In Steiner's view, causes for behavior are found both within the child and without. His emphasis is on the importance of both the environment and the teaching methodology for child development. The issue is not nature or nurture, but both.

Our temperaments are expressed by psychological and physical characteristics which fall into four broad groups: melancholic, phlegmatic, sanguine, and choleric. Each of us has the possibility of expressing ourselves through all four temperaments, but in most of us one or two dominate at a time. There is no good or bad temperament. Yet at different times the 'I' can permeate one temperament more easily than another. Depending how 'developed' we are the 'I' can achieve the highest human qualities of selflessness – regardless of our dominant temperament – while at a lower stage, the temperament may block this expression and appear to be a source of selfishness and egotism. As we develop through the major stages of life, the 'I' takes hold of our temperaments and tries to transform them. It is this development that we recognize in others when we notice how much nicer and kinder they become as they grow older.

We may say: 'That Mrs. Rollins was so pushy and aggressive, but she mellowed as she got older and now she is quite pleasant to be around.' Or: 'Mr. Hanstead was so scattered. He couldn't finish anything. But oh, he was a charming fellow! I found myself constantly making allowances for him. As he's grown older, he has become so much more reliable and responsible.' Or: 'Old Miss Stone is so gentle and kind. It's hard to believe that she was once self-pitying and stubborn.' Or we may overhear the following: 'My friend Andrew is loyal and patient with me. I am so grateful for him.' 'Oh, yes,' remarks a friend who has known Andrew since childhood, 'he wasn't so patient when he was younger. He was aloof and concerned only with himself'.

The temperament develops slowly during the earliest years of life and emerges between the fifth and seventh years. It appears most strongly from seven to fourteen years of age. At that age, the child is also the most impressionable. After fourteen, the individual becomes more conscious of how she behaves, and after twenty-one, with the birth of the 'I', the individual actively works on the temperament, consciously or unconsciously. This work goes on to the last days of our lives.

The book, *Understanding Our Fellow Men*,[2] by Danish psychologist Knud Asbjorn Lund, has been invaluable in helping me understand how the temperaments change during the major stages of life.

To understand the possibility of transforming our temperaments, let us look at life as divided into three periods:

1st stage – *Egoism or Immaturity phase*. During this first period, we basically act out of egoism. We believe that it is proper to be most concerned about ourselves (egoism), and we tend to have an exaggerated sense of our own importance (egotism). We consider ourselves the center of the world. Everything that happens in some way revolves around us. We are strongly influenced by our developing physical bodies and we identify with them.

2nd stage – *Life experience phase*. In the second stage, we acquire life experience and come to realize that we must consider others as well as ourselves. These are the great years of soul development. Our identities are connected with our feelings, thoughts, and actions, with what we experience inwardly as well as outwardly. We experience tension between what we want for ourselves and what we know is more noble and selfless.

3rd stage – *Mature phase*. In the third stage, we gain perspective from our experience and adopt a clearer and wider outlook. As we take hold of our soul life, we shape it so that it more clearly expresses our higher selves. We see that we receive more joy the more we give and and the less we demand.

Although we usually pass from the immature phase to the mature phase chronologically, some young people seem to act unselfishly as a matter of course, while some old folk still act selfishly and immaturely.

Now let us look at each of the four temperaments, remembering that most of us have more than one active temperament.

The Melancholic

1st stage – In general, melancholics are absorbed in themselves and don't take much notice of other people. Life is sad and gloomy. The melancholic demands pity, is turned inward, asks for sympathy, and has little to give to others.

2nd stage – Here the melancholic wavers between egoism and self-abnegation. She wants to be unselfish but doesn't have enough strength to maintain it and gives in to egoism. Vacillation and repeated crises mark this stage.

3rd stage – The melancholic can now see that her greatest satisfaction is in being of value to others. The more the 'melancholic' acts this way, the richer she feels.

The Phlegmatic

1st stage – Phlegmatics want to live within themselves. They live a balanced life, spurn all that is new and all that comes from outside. They are stubborn and concerned most of all with their own comfort.

2nd stage – Slowly the phlegmatic feels the needs of others. She may change, but she is resistant. She approaches anything new and unfamiliar slowly and cautiously, and then only when it is brought to her by others. She is uncomfortable with change, yet she can see that change is sometimes necessary.

3rd stage – The phlegmatic is sensitive to the needs of others as well as to her own. She is conservative, faithful, upright, honorable, and patient in carrying out her work to the last detail and in relating to fellow human beings.

The Sanguine

1st stage – The sanguine is emotional and extremely variable. She wants to come into contact with all that is new, and craves what is novel and amusing. She captivates with charm, using people for her own ends, and goes her carefree way when it suits her, leaving others to take the consequences. She starts many projects but completes few.

2nd stage – Full of good intentions but lacking the strength of character to carry through her plans, the sanguine is an impressive talker with all sorts of wonderful ideas, yet when these ideas don't materialize, she has an excuse for every situation. She is caught between wanting to have fun and wanting to be responsible.

3rd stage – By now, the sanguine has gained a degree of self-control. She is lovable, generous, and intuitive. She still enjoys the new and challenging, but now she wants the results to be helpful to other people.

The Choleric

1st stage – The choleric is stubborn and strong-willed. She insists on her own way. Opposition makes her more forceful, sometimes even brutal, in expressing her egoism. Cholerics are natural leaders, but they monopolize and intimidate.

2nd stage – The choleric shows interest in other people and realizes that they, too, have intelligence and skills. She tries to hold back, but is caught between knowing that she can do it better and respecting others. She still wants power, and convinces herself that she must keep control so that the work gets done better and more efficiently.

3rd stage – The choleric has learned to respect other people. She has become a gentle ruler who uses her skills and organizing abilities for the benefit of others. She has learned to subordinate herself and rejoices in the accomplishments of others.

Four ways of meeting life

Each season of our lives also has a quality of temperament. Childhood with its un-selfconscious egoism and joy is sanguine. Youth, with its focus on action and building the future, is choleric. Middle age, with its challenges, frustrations, and anxieties, is melancholic. Old age, with its acceptance of life and distance from ambitions and turmoils, is phlegmatic.

For the melancholic life is anxiety, for the phlegmatic it is well-being, for the sanguine an adventure, and for the choleric, work.

Chapter 2. The Melancholic Temperament: Why do the burdens of the world fall on me?

Even as children, melancholics walk with the heaviness of old people. Usually lean in build, they walk slowly and uncertainly. Typically, the melancholic's head is bent toward the earth, shoulders and face drooping. Closed within his thoughts, his voice is soft and restrained. He often mumbles and leaves sentences hanging.

The melancholic is uncomfortable in his body, feeling every ache and pain. He is hypersensitive to how his clothes fit and how different materials feel against his body. He complains of feeling unwell and lacks vitality. He is acutely aware of all his physical ailments and quite willing to describe them in great detail to anyone who will listen.

Sleep is the melancholic's refuge, and he feels that he never gets very much (even though his snoring may keep others awake). Melancholics are slow to wake up and do not like to be rushed – after all, each day only brings possibilities for more problems and especially for failure. It takes too much will power to face this dismal world, and it's exhausting to think about it. So he takes a long time getting out of bed.

Bound up within themselves, melancholics don't pay much attention to others. They are serious, quiet, withdrawn, and reflective. Their whole gesture is downward and into themselves. They live deeply in the past and in their memories, hanging onto details, unavailable to the demands of the present. A mood of sadness surrounds them.

They are sure that they carry a greater burden of life than other people and they are resigned to it. They imagine that others are trying to hurt them or make their lives miserable. They worry constantly and look for obstacles blocking their way. All kinds of catastrophes are imagined, so they fear going far from home, avoiding unfamiliar experiences because each is a potential danger. If they do travel, they remember how miserable it was. They carry guilt for what goes wrong around them and expect to be punished, even for deeds that are not their fault. That is just the way life is.

Melancholic lyrics are found in poems and songs from all over the world, depicting loneliness, loss, and isolation. In a beautiful Latvian *daina* (folksong), a young woman bewails her life isolated from her family and unhappy with her husband and inlaws. The mood epitomizes the melancholic's sense of being left out (which, in this case, may be a reality.)

> *Like a stone into a creek*
> *I am thrown among strangers*
> *Never came Mama to visit,*
> *No brother came to check on me,*
> *Has some pine tree or fir tree*
> *Fallen across the road to block me in?*
> *On the white feet of a ram*
> *I go to visit my brothers.*
> *Little quail shows me the path*
> *A wild duck tracks through the dew.*
> *Ai, maminya, beloved and pure,*
> *Difficult is my life with these people.*
> *Sharp and harsh my husband's mother,*
> *And a heart of wood has her son.* [1]

Everyone has melancholic moods at times, but those with a strong melancholic temperament have difficulty letting go of them. Their thoughts become fixed and they find it difficult to change their position or point of view. Doing so would mean stepping outside themselves and becoming objective. They cannot see that they might be wrong, and, taking themselves so seriously, they cannot laugh at themselves. Making decisions is painful. Often they sigh deeply and respond in a toneless voice. When finally they do act, it is usually too slowly and inappropriately.

Melancholics are the classic perfectionists, meticulous workers who expect their work to be flawless. When the melancholic makes a mistake, however, it confirms his sense that he is a failure and he destroys the work. Therefore, melancholics leave many things unfinished and carry the burden of these 'failures' in their minds, often reminding themselves that it isn't worth making an effort since the result won't be good anyway. Facing a huge task, they can become paralyzed.

Yet, if a melancholic becomes interested in a project, he can give himself completely to it. He is capable of deep pondering and exhaustive research. He has tremendous energy at his disposal, and leaves no stone unturned. Meticulousness serves him well. Melancholics often produce original solutions.

It is difficult for the melancholic to make friends. Generally, he is a loner, with only one or two trusted friends. To these friends he is loyal and true – but if he feels that his friend has betrayed him, he is wounded for life. He can speak at length with people who share his interests, but he has little use for others and looks with disdain at those who flit about, touching into life in a superficial way. Because he lacks humor and is easily annoyed, other children (or adults) may be drawn to tease him. He can't stand this and it only confirms his feeling that the world is an unfriendly place.

As adults, melancholics are on the look-out for confirmation that they are worthless and that life will disappoint them. For example, a group of friends may mention to a melancholic that they are going skiing, but they don't specifically say, 'We are going on January 20th at 8 a.m. We very much want you to come with us.'

The melancholic waits to be asked again – but it doesn't happen. He is sure that there is a reason behind this and concludes that he is not really wanted, feels self-pity, and begins to store up anger toward the friends.

'They planned it this way. Why would they mention it and then not ask me to come? They didn't really want me to come.' So the melancholic goes into a tailspin that may climax in a full-fledged depression.

The melancholic is always expecting to find that he or she is not as good as others, so it doesn't take more than a slight misunderstanding or lack of sensitivity on the part of others for this feeling to be substantiated. Friends and partners of melancholics need to be very specific when inviting them, and to warmly encourage them to join them. They may even need to cajole, but it is worth it. The melancholic very much wants to be included but doesn't have the courage to ask, for fear of being turned down.

Melancholics can be kind and gentle. They are longing for sympathy and when someone gives it to them, they will be loyal in return. But they may go too far and overwhelm the sympathetic person with their tales of woe, often testing his patience beyond endurance. Without realizing what he is doing, the melancholic, in his pickiness, may point out faults in how the other person is helping him and become grouchy and seemingly unappreciative. The other person is left feeling that nothing is ever enough. With this behavior, the melancholic may drive away the very person who is showing him kindness.

The melancholic mood may seem more characteristic of people in middle or old age who have objective experiences to feel melancholic about, but not of children whose lives are ahead of them. That is why melancholic children have such a hard time. They don't seem to fit.

In the first stage, melancholics are concerned only about themselves. Their egoism cuts them off from other people even though, deep inside, they long to do something for others. Because aspects of all three stages are present all the time, we see children and adolescents whose melancholic temperament enables them to show a depth of sympathy and caring to an old person, a wounded animal, or a person who has experienced disappointment and pain. At such moments, the melancholic forgets his own woes. Because he understands suffering, he is grateful to meet other people who also understand it.

From the first to the second stage

Sympathy is the turning point from the first stage to the second. When a melancholic feels sympathy for another human being, he ceases to be an egoist. In taking interest in others, he moves out of his egoism. Similarly, when he becomes deeply interested in a hobby or project, he forgets himself. Then he is quite happy to help those who need advice and have patience and tolerance for them. When common interests create a bridge, the melancholic can be an excellent conversationalist.

In the second stage, melancholics still have a difficult time. They experience sympathy and understanding for others. They overcome their egoism at certain times, but the battle between their egoism and their unselfishness continues. Such battle causes constant crisis between the lower and higher selves of the melancholic individual.

It is not unusual for the melancholic to feel that life's opportunities are passing him by. In a mood of self-pity, he may reach out for positions of responsibility. Unfortunately, his temperament works against him unless he has completely transformed himself. He may feel that he is not getting enough help from co-workers, that subordinates are plotting against him, that he has been set up to fail. He may spend hours bewailing his fate to those who will listen. After a while, even friends become fed up with it.

Several things help the melancholic deal with these situations. When he starts talking about himself and his troubles, it doesn't help if he is ignored. That only confirms his loneliness. What helps is, firstly, for someone to ask him questions – and then, after he has given enough of an answer so that the picture is clear, quickly move to another aspect, and then another. Then the melancholic doesn't get stuck. He gets to tell his tale of woe but he has to cut it short. After a while, he is talked out and has nothing more to say. He feels contented and satisfied. Then, if the friend goes on and asks even more questions so that the melancholic has nothing more to add, this helps him move away from his egoism.

If melancholics are allowed to take advantage of their friends, they can become manipulative. They may even become tyrants. Friends and family members have to know when to draw the line and say, 'Enough is enough.' People misinterpret melancholics as being so fragile that they cannot accept being confronted, but quite the opposite is true. They need these boundaries. Otherwise their egoism is fed and they are unable to go beyond it to develop further.

Life for the untransformed melancholic can be fraught with anxiety and self-pity. He is often ill and leaves things undone because he feels so unwell. The mood in the house is heavy. Everyone suffers under the melancholic's depressions. The quiet is not a peaceful quiet but a burdensome one.

On the other hand, in the homes of other, more developed melancholics, the mood may be gentle and kind. On one wall is a collection of miniatures, all well dusted. A pile of books sits on a table for the melancholic's life-long research project. (Never mind that the cat's dish is covered with typing paper! This research is very important and takes concentration.) There may be several boxes with wounded birds which are being cared for, fed every thirty-five minutes. Plants are treated with love and attention, as if they were tender children. It is always interesting to visit. Sometimes we are offered tea; other times, hours may go by while our host tells us about his work or how he feels. He may even forget to ask us to sit down. His halting and quiet voice may make us think that he is in pain, but actually, he is having a wonderful time.

Rather than constantly feeling sorry for the melancholic and sympathizing with him, ask him to do something for you. Don't be afraid to make demands. He may at first list all the things he has to do and explain why he has no time. He may feel that the demand is impossible to accomplish. When he takes it on, however, he is grateful for the opportunity to sacrifice himself for someone else. Even if he sees someone else's need, he will seldom volunteer to do something to help, but if there is a direct request he is forced to respond one way or another, and he is pleased. What the melancholic most deeply longs for is to sacrifice himself, even though his personal egoism tries to prevent this. If he is constantly given his own way, this feeds his egoism. Being given an opportunity to perform selfless acts is an even greater gift for the melancholic than for others.

A big step comes if he gives in to another person or sees an opportunity to help and does it. Then he feels much better because deep in his heart he knows that his life has real value only when he does something for others. This marks the transition to the third stage.

But even after he recognizes this, the battle between his two natures goes on. Should I reach out to others, or should I hold back? If others do not understand this, if they do not create situations where the sympathy of the melancholic is aroused, then the melancholic will relapse and his egoism take over. We have to expect ups and downs in this struggle. In fits of depression the melancholic may break off contact with people who have labored to get through to him. 'It won't matter anyway,' he tells himself, wanting to punish others by hurting himself. 'They'll cry at my funeral,' or 'I'll show them. I'll hurt myself; then they'll be sorry they treated me this way.'

It is easy to misunderstand the actions of the melancholic. For example, he may say no when he means yes. Why? Because he wants to be begged or persuaded. He wants to be sure that he is really, really needed. He may complain that he doesn't feel so well, that he doesn't have time, but if these excuses are accepted and the person making the request goes away, the melancholic is left feeling disappointed and even resentful. Friends of melancholics need to walk a fine line between being persistent and being unreasonable. When a melancholic develops a circle of friends who understand him and whom he trusts, this is a great achievement. It is difficult for melancholics to completely overcome their egoism and move into the third stage, which is total self-sacrifice.

Stage three

The third stage is reached when the battle is clearly won (with some room for occasional relapse). The melancholic now has far more interest in others than in himself. His life has been placed in the service of others. In this, he finds his true meaning. At this stage, the melancholic is a gentle, caring, loving human being. His earlier pessimism has been transformed. He no longer waits for a direct request to help. He is able to show appreciation to others. In other words, he rises above his egoism and is able to suffer for others. This is then transformed into conscious self-sacrifice for other people.

Variants of the melancholic

When a melancholic has sanguine tendencies also, he has moments of lightness in which he can laugh at himself and during which he can feel joy and optimism. His sanguine side can help him occasionally enjoy social situations and pull him out of his self-involvement. But not for long.

If a melancholic has strong choleric tendencies, this may re-inforce his egoism, prompting him to break into rages and giving him the energy to seek revenge. However, when melancholics overcome their egoism, their choleric tendencies help them to carry their interests into life, finishing projects and sharing with others.

A melancholic often sees the fearful side of life. For example, Rema warned everyone about walking on the streets at night. When questioned about the 'many, many attacks' which she said were going on in the neighborhood, she could remember only one incident – from her childhood. But she still carried the fear within her, feeling that danger was present all the time. If there was a light snow, she imagined ice on the streets, cars crashing into each other. If one friend lost his job, she was sure that she would, too. When faced with interviews for promotions, she was sure that she would fail. When faced with a small rent increase, she imagined that her family would be driven from their home. Life was perceived as a threat.

Alexandra warned her friends how difficult and dangerous it was to travel to a particular country. They would be attacked and robbed. It was very very expensive. They would not be able to relax and enjoy themselves. She worried terribly that they were making a wrong decision and tried to dissuade them from going.

Luckily, in the cases of both Rema and Alexandra, aspects of other temperaments were also working strongly so that they were not overcome by their strong melancholic tendencies. Both were highly capable and warm human beings who loved life and people, but each had enough of a melancholic streak to see the world from that vantage point and at times was overwhelmed by it.

Olaf, a melancholic engineer, was faced with writing a long report. He complained to himself that it was too much to ask, that he would never finish. The longer he did this, the more he convinced himself that he could not do it. Soon he was paralyzed and could not even begin. The situation became so problematical that he put his job in jeopardy, managing to keep it only because friends stepped in firmly and stayed with him while he worked on the report. He was very grateful for the help, but it also confirmed to him that he had a terrible problem. At home, he complained of all that he had to do, but spent his evenings slumped in front of the television.

It was the request of a close friend who asked him to help him build a house over the summer that helped snap Olaf out of his slump. He earned some much-needed extra money, but more than that, he had the daily companionship of a supportive friend who enjoyed building and enjoyed Olaf. Making jokes, taking a break for a few minutes to play basketball, and long summer days in the fresh air all helped. At the end of each day, Olaf had good reason to be tired, and he hadn't spent the hours feeling sorry for himself. He had something specific every day that he had accomplished. He was helping a friend and he was helping himself.

Grace was torn between generosity and self-pity. She loved to give gifts and she had spent time finding just the one that her son would love. But when he didn't respond positively enough (in her expectations), she felt that her energy had been wasted, that she wasn't appreciated, and that she wouldn't do it again. Luckily, her black mood didn't last too long and she was able to talk herself out of it.

Martin was working from the second stage to the third stage of his melancholic temperament. He was recently retired and had been encouraged to volunteer to visit old people in a nearby nursing home. At first, he was willing to go once a week, and he played chess with some of the residents. In listening to their problems, he discovered they had worse troubles than he did, and he started going every day. He wrote letters for them and found different ways to cheer them up. His gentleness and sweet smile permeated that wing of the nursing home and the workers looked forward to his visits. Each day when he walked out of the lobby, he felt that he was fulfilling his ideals.

Melancholic women often go through major changes after their children have grown. What next? Whom will they fuss over? Ellen was married to a sweet phlegmatic man, and between them there was hardly ever a voice raised. She had cultivated many interests during those years and loved music, poetry, art, and cooking. She had a few close friends, several dogs, and a wonderfully productive garden. She had never taken a leading role in anything, but had always been quite happy to help in her children's school. Yet when people met her, they had the impression of a meek person who could hardly keep a steady gaze.

When her youngest child finished school, Ellen did what she had always wanted to do. She began training to be a kindergarten teacher. Now all her talents would have an outlet. She was a mature melancholic, with all the loveliness of the temperament. Her sensitivity to others would make her a fine colleague. Her gentleness would be comforting to the little children. Beneath her tenderness was strength which would stand her in good stead with the rascally ones. She would bring the best of herself to her new career.

Emily's situation was a little different. She had been married for over twenty-five years to a choleric husband. Next to her husband's strength she felt weak. Whereas sanguines usually enjoy being around cholerics, melancholics are intimidated by them. Every year, it seemed that Emily became more and more withdrawn as she felt less and less worthy. She stopped caring how she looked. She ignored her hobbies. She felt that she wasn't capable of following a career after her children left home. She became depressed and saw a doctor. Then a strange thing happened. Emily's husband left her. At first, she went even more deeply into depression. She didn't know how she would survive the divorce. But after several months, she began to come out of it. Now, for the first time, she felt really free. She began to see her life from a new perspective. Her husband was no longer there to boss her around. She could spend her time as she wanted.

Earlier in her life, Emily had had a great love of botany and zoology. She decided now to go back to the university for the degree which she had never finished. At first, this was very frightening, but each day she made herself go through the paces. She enrolled in the classes and loved her studies. She became stronger and more confident every day. As Emily flowered in her studies, she also began doing things which she had never had the confidence to do. She backpacked by herself, took field trips to faraway places, and discovered how much she enjoyed being with people as well as by herself. She lost the weight which she had put on during those last ten years of marriage, and she began to enjoy the way she looked. After completing her studies, she founded an institute for rescuing wounded animals, organized groups to clean birds after an oil spill, and trained teenagers how to set broken wings of birds. Her patience and attention to detail helped her in this work. She had not only transformed her temperament, but had discovered other aspects of herself (other temperament tendencies) which had been hiding all those years.

The transformed melancholic is a great gift to humanity.

Chapter 3. The Phlegmatic Temperament: Everything's fine. Don't rock the boat

Like melancholics, phlegmatics also turn inward. Where the melancholic experiences the burdens of the world, however, the phlegmatic has a sense of well-being. Phlegmatics typically have a roundness and heaviness to their bodies. They move slowly and deliberately, their muscles tend to have a flabby tone. They live in the fluid element, being most affected by the glandular activity of their bodies. Their outer appearance can be misleading as their eyes seem to be dull and lack interest. They look calm, rather than pained like the melancholic. Their voice is clear but without much change of tone. They tend to go on and on without a lot of drama. What they say is usually correct but rather boring. They want to give a complete answer and become annoyed if they are cut off before they finish. They walk with a long unhurried stride. Their loose and heavy limbs can be clumsy, and they do not like to exert themselves.

They are concerned with the comforts of life. Creatures of routine and habit, they want their meals at the same time every day because it makes sense. Food is very important and they eat heartily. Not very interested in trying out new tastes, they have old favorites to which they are loyal. Their homes need to be simple and comfortable with good light, and nice places to curl up for a nap. When a phlegmatic is established in her favorite armchair, she can sit for hours. The phlegmatic has a regular rhythm of waking and sleeping and falls quickly asleep. She becomes disgruntled if this rhythm is broken by outer events.

Everything about phlegmatics suggests time. They move comparatively slowly and dislike any kind of haste. This gives an outer, but usually false impression that they are lazy. They are sluggish, deliberate, and somewhat 'asleep'. When they set about a task, they take time to set everything out, to be sure they understand what they have to do, and, most of all, they need time to work things out carefully. They will slowly come to a decision about how to go about a task. Once they start, however, they are very orderly and reliable. They will persevere in the minutest detail, and don't want to stop. They can tackle only one job at a time. They don't mind routine work because it is familiar to them. They can do the same task over and over again without being bored.

Some phlegmatics are not very affected by their environment and can function in the midst of total chaos. As long as their needs are met, the phlegmatic just doesn't notice the chaos. She is functioning within the order of her inner world. Hardly aware of what is going on around her, she is comfortable as long as other people don't interfere.

Like melancholics, phlegmatics are turned in on themselves. They like to dream and take things easy. They enjoy life but don't get too bothered about it. For this reason, they are very stubborn and do not like change. Once they have accepted change, however, they want to keep things as they are once more. They are always most happy in the status quo, which they accept as natural. They don't anxiously pace the floor as the melancholic might, worrying that a spouse or child might have suffered a car accident or that the mole on their arm is really cancer. The phlegmatic's attitude is, 'What will happen will happen, so there's no sense worrying.'

Anecdote: Michael

Michael is a phlegmatic. Even-tempered and pleasant, he nonetheless is having frustrations at work. He doesn't speak about it – but he gets an ulcer. He doesn't want to rock the boat and complain. It takes much badgering from his wife for him to go to the doctor, and then he refuses to take his medicine.

Although phlegmatics learn slowly, they learn well. They are slow to respond, however – and it seems that cholerics and sanguines never want to allow them enough time. The phlegmatic needs to dig deeply into his memory to find some bit of information. Once he finds it, however, he finds a richness of detail to go with it.

Phlegmatics are conservative in their behavior. They are sensible and rather old-fashioned in everything they do. They won't change their ways without a very convincing reason and, even then, they won't change quickly. What has been done before is fine. Before making a decision, the phlegmatic must consider all aspects. Decisions cannot be rushed. If she goes to buy something, it is because it is needed, not just for the sake of a change. For example, a phlegmatic's spouse may suggest buying new curtains or a new car.

'Why?' she is likely to reply, 'is there a problem with what we have already?'

If asked, 'Dear, what can I buy you for your birthday?' the phlegmatic wife replies, 'I don't need anything. Everything I have still works.' (That includes the favorite sweater that is twenty-five years old and has been patched several times.) A good gift may be a favorite coffee or tea, or a special kind of chocolate or sausage.

A phlegmatic's life is usually well organized. What has been broken is repaired, papers are organized and filed, bills are paid on time, tools are kept sharpened and hanging properly where they can always be found.

When a phlegmatic is surrounded by a mess, it is usually because she needs lots of time to organize and there's never enough time. Unlike sanguines or cholerics, who can do a bit here or there in an available hour, the phlegmatic needs to put things in order before tackling the task itself. By the time she has organized herself, the hour is gone. If she doesn't think there is enough time to complete the task properly, she may decide not even to begin.

On the job, she prefers not to assert herself. She would rather carry out other people's orders than give orders herself. In fact, phlegmatics have great difficulty being leaders. Modest in their demeanor, they can't see themselves trying to make other people do things. The phlegmatic is saddened that other people rush around to get things done, when she knows that such rushing would not be necessary if only they would live and let live.

If you try to hurry a phlegmatic, she digs in her heels and resists. She doesn't argue – she just doesn't move. It is as if she didn't hear. Finally, she will try to keep peace by doing the absolute minimum, but only after exasperating everyone around.

As part of her conservative view of life, the phlegmatic takes everything literally. You cannot expect her to respond to unspoken assumptions, subtlety, or unspoken expectations. What you ask for is what you get. This is not at all a lack of good will. In fact, a phlegmatic is full of good will. Nonetheless, people often find the phlegmatic exasperating because of her stubborn, immovable nature.

Anecdote: Celia

A rather humorous event occurred with Celia, a typical phlegmatic. She was big and strong and liked her comforts. One day, she finished her work as a department store shoe-saleswoman and took the bus home. She was very tired and her feet ached. She stepped into the elevator and pushed the button for her floor. But a young man quickly stepped into the elevator, and, keeping the door open with one leg, he demanded her purse. She was insulted and began to tell him how hard she had worked and how her feet hurt. She offered to show him the corns on her feet. She stood at the far corner of the elevator like a rock and refused to hand him her purse. She had just enough mixture of phlegmatic and melancholic that she stood her ground but continued to tell him the long story of how hard she worked for the little money she earned. The thief finally gave up and left.

In a group, it is quite easy to overlook phlegmatics, but they themselves are great observers. They watch without getting involved. When they do comment, the remark is usually droll and to the point. They use their wit both as protection and as a weapon, because they don't like to shift or move. Danish psychologist Lund describes the following scene:

> In married life the Phlegmatic has his own special peculiarities. He feels that it is his duty to do his best, in order that he and his family shall have as nice a home as possible. However, he not infrequently marries a woman who, lacking his psychological insight, assumes that his achievements will be in proportion to his size. In this she is liable to be disappointed. He has no objection to rising first in the

morning and giving her a cup of tea in bed. In fact, he is an early riser by nature – and in any case he wants her to be comfortable.

It is also easy for her to enlist his aid on washing day … When the Phlegmatic comes home from work his wife is bursting to tell him all about the events of her day. She chatters away happily until it is all out. For his part, he is quite content to listen, as long as he is not expected to talk. The meal is prepared quickly, and the wife is looking forward to hearing all about his day – but when it comes to the point, he has absolutely nothing to tell her. He had not noticed the lunch she had been at such pains to prepare for him. Nothing particular happened at the office. What his boss thinks of this or that is no concern of his. He had not heard the witticisms of his comrades. He has nothing to say.

Disappointed, the wife goes off to the kitchen to wash up, and standing there at the sink alone, she begins to wonder if he has ceased to care for her. She hastens back to the sitting-room to ask him if he still loves her. But she gets no answer to her question, for he is fast asleep on the sofa. If she wakes him up, he only rumbles sleepily, and when she suggests that they might go to the cinema, he yawns, 'Oh, not tonight – I really can't be bothered.'

She sticks to her guns. How about going round to the Smiths, then? Or asking the Joneses in for a game of Whist. Or why not go out for a little walk?

He turns down all her bright ideas, until in desperation she suggests that they go to bed. With a happy, drowsy smile he answers, 'Yes, let's – and have a good sleep.' [1]

This kind of phlegmatic can drive his wife to distraction. If she were phlegmatic, too, they would just enjoy their sedentary life together, but if she is not, she is constantly trying to find some way to get him moving. He, however – a first stage phlegmatic – cares only about his own comfort.

It is not unusual for phlegmatics to marry cholerics or sanguines. It is interesting for them to have activity around them, as long as they do not have to take the initiative. However, there are problems ahead.

Anecdotes: Rachel, Patricia, Philip, Ron

Rachel, for instance, was married to a very pleasant phlegmatic. She herself was a very active sanguine-choleric and loved to socialize. She kept waiting for her husband to suggest that they go to a restaurant, but he never did. She grew angrier and angrier and protested to a friend, 'I always have to suggest that we do something. I'm tired of it!'

She continued to wait. Still, nothing happened. Finally, she burst out with all kinds of accusations. 'Don't you care? Don't you ever want to have a good time? Do you not want to be with me? You're making me so unhappy!'

Tom was startled. He thought that everything was fine. He liked being home and didn't particularly need to go out. He thought that Rachel was happy, too, since she hadn't said anything. This precipitated a conversation which was very helpful. Once Tom understood the problem, he was able to say, 'Look Rachel, I love being with you, and I'm very happy when we are both at home, puttering around, relaxing, having a cup of tea together. I like that. And I have no problem going out to dinner or to a movie with you if you would like to go, but I never think about it. If you want to go, just tell me, and I'll happily go, or, if I really don't want to, I'll tell you.'

This was extremely helpful for Rachel. She realized that he wasn't doing anything to hurt her or ignore her. He had no intentions at all. It simply didn't occur to him. She stopped expecting something that she now realized was unreasonable to expect. She found that she did more things herself, went out with friends, and if she wanted to go somewhere with Tom, she asked him directly and he usually enjoyed going.

This is not the case with phlegmatic husbands only. The situation is often reversed. Patricia was a jolly sort of phlegmatic woman with many interests and friends. But she had the phlegmatic's inwardness and dreaminess, especially in her soul life. Her husband Zack was a choleric-sanguine who was very proud of his cleverness. He learned that when he made sarcastic remarks, Patricia just took them. She didn't strike back as a choleric would, and she didn't lapse into tears as a melancholic would. She just took it. He began to criticise her in front of the children and in front of friends. He stung her with his barbs. She felt uncomfortable but didn't know why. Patricia did not consciously realize that Zack was really hurting her, but she had a nagging sense of unease. She took refuge in her own thoughts and activities.

Then a friend told her that she was uncomfortable in Patricia's house because of the way Zack treated her. Patricia vaguely understood what her friend was saying. Then another friend mentioned it as well. Patricia began to wake up a little, and the next time Zack threw a sarcastic remark her way, she thought, 'He really is doing this. I have been feeling that something wasn't right, but I didn't know what it was.' It took Patricia about five years to feel strongly enough to say something to Zack. By then, his habit had become a way of life, and he denied that he was hurting her. He said that she was just thin-skinned. Imagine! As Patricia woke up to her situation, her anger became stronger and stronger. She divorced Zack and he never could figure out why.

Philip told me that he had been an extreme phlegmatic as a child and everyone had just left him alone. He didn't learn much at school and didn't do much at all, even at home. He was pleasant and not a troublemaker, so he was left to vegetate. In his twenties, he woke up and realized all that he had missed. He was very angry to think of those wasted years. He pleaded with me to tell people that they must force phlegmatics to shake off their lethargy, even if they don't like it. Teachers and parents need to get their attention and cause them to be active and be responsible for learning what is being taught.

If phlegmatics are annoyed or badgered too much, however, look out! They will eventually rouse themselves with tremendous force into a powerful rage, and once they start, it isn't easy for them to stop. When they are forced to act quickly, they get muddled, and in some situations, behave irrationally.

Ron was respected and enjoyed for his good nature. He was a good worker and loyal to his organization. Everyone relied on him, and he managed things well. Every once in a while, however, he erupted, after which he was his sweet, good-natured self for months again.

Stage one

Phlegmatics in the first stage express their egoism by wanting to live comfortably within themselves. All that I have described about them is their need to feel good and balanced. Laurence, for example, has a wonderful, full laugh. His friends feel secure near him. He has just enough sanguinity in his personality to be light and funny, but he is also predictable enough that one can rely on him in any circumstance. He is at peace with himself.

Stage two

The transition to the second stage occurs when the phlegmatic experiences something new and considers making a change. The change does not rise out of herself, but is brought upon her by others. At first, she is very cautious, but slowly she becomes willing to consider it.

To help phlegmatics make this change, we must approach them gently. We cannot give them orders, because they will resist them. They are especially responsive to watching the way other people do things and then copying them. They will carefully observe every detail. Phlegmatics don't lack intelligence; they lack initiative. However, after they have watched someone else complete a task, and given enough time, they may come up with a better way. But they must be left in peace while they work on it.

Anecdotes: Aaron, Ruth

For example, Aaron typifies a phlegmatic approach to work. He has a position in a public relations firm. His approach to his assignments is careful and slow. Step by step he develops each advertising program. He doesn't have any flashes of insight. He plods along. In another office, his colleagues are coming up with exciting new projects, impulsive attempts at attracting attention for their clients. But not our phlegmatic friend! Steady but sure, he continues along his way. One day, however, he wanders into the other office and sees what his colleagues are doing. They have laid out their plan in a new way, which he studies carefully. Over the next few days, he sees new possibilities in his own plan. He works on it for several weeks and finds ways to improve it and make it even better.

Ruth is another example. She enjoys making craft projects, but has no initiative to start them herself. She likes to visit a friend who is very creative and always working on something interesting. When Ruth is with her friend, she is very active and enjoys making many things. She finds new ways to cut patterns and finish seams and spends hours working meticulously while her faster-working friend has already moved on to other projects. Ruth finishes her one project and has done it very well, but she won't begin another project on her own.

In the second stage, phlegmatics vacillate between old comforts and new situations. Left to themselves, they do not go beyond what feels good to them. They repeat themselves over and over, stuck in their old ways. They have to learn from others how to take interest in other people and in their surroundings. If a phlegmatic respects someone else, she will be loyal and true and will learn from that person. Through this relationship, the phlegmatic begins to move out into the world. In this stage, phlegmatics will attend social gatherings, even enjoy them, as long as there is no pressure on them to perform. Deep in their hearts, they long to do new things. By giving them the chance to copy something or to participate socially, we are helping the phlegmatics bring out new parts of their character. When they have new experiences which they like, they are grateful for the kindness and are devoted to the person who helps them overcome their reticence and shyness. Of course, there are relapses – times when phlegmatics don't feel like exerting themselves.

Anecdotes: Arturo, Susan, Donald, Carol

Whereas their tenacity can help them, it can also alienate them from others. Arturo, a bookkeeper, volunteered to do the books for an organization he supported. He worked long and hard, but when other volunteers questioned his approach, he sulked, feeling that they didn't appreciate all the time he was putting in. He was so careful about every detail. Co-workers said that he was being fanatical in interpreting the law in the tightest possible way, but, in his view, he was trying to be consistent,while they were trying to get away with something. He knew that he was right and he would not budge, but he wouldn't discuss it with them. He avoided the situation by deciding not to volunteer his services anymore.

Susan is even-tempered and jolly about life, but she was unhappy about some things at work. She didn't know what could be be done, but when someone presented a plan that seemed to solve the problem, she took hold of it. She brought it up at every opportunity. The group decided to implement it. After several months it became clear that the plan was flawed, and the person who had presented it withdrew it. Susan drove her colleagues to distraction by continually raising the issue. Although she had no suggestion to improve the plan, she wouldn't let go. Stuck in the second stage, she went back and forth between what she wanted in the past and what would be needed for the future. She liked the plan because it served her needs. Only slowly did she see that the plan didn't meet other people's needs. In those moments, she was lifted out of her egoism.

In the second stage, phlegmatics enjoy sharing their sense of well-being wth others. For instance, Ivan, who lives in the former Soviet Union where food has been scarce, goes from store to store until he finds a sausage. With a chuckle, he presents it to the family and invites everyone to enjoy it. Jason, another second-stage phlegmatic, makes a hobby of collecting train schedules. It gives him great pleasure when he can help others by providing them with all the various (and best) ways to travel. However, he goes on and on, flooding his listeners with more information than they can possibly deal with. His help may be tiresome, but Jason is acting with the intention of helping.

Stage three

In the third stage, the phlegmatic is sensitive to other people's needs. She is a trusted, honoured member of society. In her secure, conservative approach to life, she is faithful, upright, and reliable. She is thorough. She carefully plans her life and it works out. Her calm and thoughtfulness are comfortable for others to be around. Her devotion to her work inspires younger workers, and she teaches less experienced co-workers how to do their tasks well. She especially appreciates being asked for suggestions and enjoys showing how to do something properly – as long as there is enough time to explain it well. She is concerned about other people's comforts and is a considerate hostess. She knows the finer things of life and enjoys talking about them and sharing them.

Phlegmatics know how to relax. They exude peace and quiet, order and rhythm. Many of the qualities which we associate with the later years of life are also characteristic of phlegmatics in stage three. They accept life and enjoy it the best way they can. Through their devotion, they bring many blessings to those around them.

I think of Carol as 'the mother of all phlegmatics'. Children gather round her, charmed and comforted by her even-temper, her attention to all the little things that make them feel happy and nurtured. Her presence alone brings a feeling of peace and security. She takes problems in her stride and keeps them at a distance.

Chapter 4. The Sanguine Temperament: I'm having a great time, but why can't I finish anything?

In contrast to the melancholic and phlegmatic temperaments, the sanguine and choleric are focused outward. The sanguine is an airy temperament. Everything about it points upward and outward. In physical appearance, the typical sanguine has a light, well proportioned body. Hands and feet are slender and well formed. Sanguines walk lightly, often running instead of walking. Sanguine children often walk on tip-toes, their feet barely touching the ground. When they sit, sanguines often put their feet up on the desk or table, or they sit sideways with legs dangling over the side. Their faces are bright and intelligent-looking, their eyes light up, and they smile easily. Their speech is quick and varied, giving rise to many different expressions. They enjoy the sound of their own voices and often chatter away, just to hear themselves talk, whether or not anyone is listening. With flitting movements, their hands often touch their necks, their faces, or their hair. Sanguines find each new experience an adventure. Like little birds, they hop about, briefly land on a surface, then disappear as quickly.

Sanguines have a tendency to be nervous. They quickly grasp impressions, but lose them just as quickly. Concentration is difficult because almost anything going on nearby will distract them. Sanguines mix their emotions with facts, making it difficult for them to be objective. When they try to be objective, they often exaggerate freely and unapologetically. Then they catch themselves, smile, and try again.

Memory is evasive, as the sanguine often cannot hold on to a thought long enough to try to find it. 'Oh, what was that?' he exclaims with momentary exasperation – but then is on to something else. As he tries to think about many different things at once, his concentration becomes fragmented and he loses the connection between thoughts. Unlike the phlegmatic, who gets stuck on thoughts and has trouble bringing them into movement, the sanguine can't hold his in focus. As he moves from thing to thing, he enjoys the excitement of the new, the changeable. 'Here today, gone tomorrow!' is his motto. He finds repetition boring and consciously tries to avoid it. If he's done something once, he figures that he has gotten everything out of it there is to get. 'Been there, done that!' is another motto. He's ready to move on.

How do sanguines relate to the physical environment? They often like to have beautiful things around, which they can arrange. They enjoy variety. They like their things, but they aren't very attached to them, often losing them. However, they don't even notice when something is missing and seem surprised when their misplaced items don't magically reappear when they need them.

Friendship is their forte. They smile and laugh and enjoy social life. They are charming and are comfortable making small talk. Nothing is boring. There is so much to see and do. But their fickleness causes them problems, as each friend thinks that he or she is the 'best' friend. Groups tend to form around the sanguine, who has so many good ideas and makes everything so exciting. Sanguines bring sunshine wherever they go, but they also tax the patience of others because they are so forgetful and unreliable. In contrast to phlegmatics, who are loyal in relationships, the sanguine is unreliable and fickle, finding it difficult to commit very long to a relationship. However, his ability to focus on the outside world gives the sanguine the capacity to put himself in another person's place. Intuitively, he understands other people and is very good at figuring out who should meet whom, who should sit next to whom at a party, and what you are trying to say – and are taking too long to do so!

When he is upset, the sanguine may flare up and say things he doesn't really mean. This soon passes, however, and he holds no grudge. He forgives easily – and expects to be forgiven. He cannot understand why a friend wants to settle past misunderstandings before resuming their relationship. His moods swing from the heights of euphoria to the depths of seeming depression, but this, too, doesn't last long.

Because the sanguine is focused outwards so strongly, he depends on the environment for stimulus. In an effort to make an impression, he concentrates on his outer image, on the latest fashion, on novelty, even on eccentricity. He follows the trend rather than depending on his own true feelings. Finding it difficult to live out of his inner resources, he depends on others. His eccentricity may be taken as individuality, but, on further examination, we see that it is merely copying the latest trend. He waxes eloquent, exaggerating, hatching one or another scheme, always sure that this is the 'sure bet', but he doesn't think things through and is often gullibly misled. Over and over, his optimism leads him into difficult situations.

Change is the joy of sanguines. It brings such wonderful possibilities. Moving, traveling, redecorating, guests, new restaurants, new friends – everything is possible and interesting. They are flexible to the nth degree.

Their behavior at work depends completely on their kind of job. If it requires talking to people, making contacts, making an impression, they are superb, but if they have to be at work at the same time every day, if they have to organize their papers and their projects, they are often hopeless. They can't remember where they file things. Sometimes a sanguine will point to a messy stack of papers, reach over and pull out the exact paper he is looking for, but this cannot be counted on regularly. They find it difficult to apply consistent rules to situations and their dealings with people, and may change them according to their mood that day. Sanguines are the great 'ideas' people. Their enthusiasm is contagious, and they can sell anything. Sanguines would rather talk than work. If they have reliable staff to carry things out for them, they make very creative members of their profession. They intuit new possibilities and celebrate innovation, but they can also find themselves unemployed because of unreliability.

Stage one

A stage one sanguine lacks the will to finish things. It is difficult for him to learn from experience, because he doesn't stop long enough to reflect. In fact, he tries to escape any kind of contemplation or reflection. He lives only in the moment. Impatience is his undoing. He cannot stay with anything. Superficial rather than profound, he knows a little bit about a lot of things, which makes a good first impression, but there's little depth.

In stage one, the sanguine's characteristics serve his egoism. He lives totally out of his feelings and wants to be the center of the world. If he hurts someone along the way ... well, he didn't intend to. He's quick to say he's sorry and promises to do better tomorrow. But tomorrow is the same. He changes his mind often and his moods quickly. He wants to be everywhere and the first to do everything. He craves all that is new and fun. If someone else is left to finish a task or carry a responsibility, that's life. He gives lots of excuses in his charming way, and it's difficult to stay angry with him. Sanguines often manipulate people for their own ends, and, because they make such superficial connections with people, they often fail to feel the suffering they cause.

The moodiness of the sanguine can be difficult to bear when life is going against them. Rather than dig in and analyze what is going wrong or focusing his energy on redoing a task, he impatiently gives up, expecting others to take care of him. He withdraws into selfishness.

Managing time is very difficult for the sanguine. He chronically does too many things at once and is usually late. If something more interesting comes up, he may forget about his next appointment. However, he offers a good excuse and tries to reschedule the appointment.

The sanguine brings forth new ideas constantly, without giving people time to digest them. Impatient with his colleagues or spouse, the sanguine becomes petulant if he doesn't get his way. But if someone likes his ideas, then that person is marvelous, the best, the most fantastic. The sanguine will do all kinds of nice things for that person – until that, too, grows boring, and there is someone else who is more marvelous. Because the sanguine makes judgments based on the moment, these are often unreliable. In the same way, he makes promises which don't mean anything the next day. He wants to feel good by tasting all the pleasures of life, by having a good time, by collecting experiences.

All of these egoistic aspects of the sanguine create a whirlwind atmosphere, but deep in the sanguine's heart is the desire to bring order to life. To do that, his will-power must be strengthened. It would seem quite natural for us to want to hold the sanguine's feet to the fire and insist on jobs being finished. This can work only when the sanguine feels that we like him. If he feels unappreciated or unaccepted, he will not change and, on the contrary, may become even more devious. Because he is so good at taking on a role and quickly changing it, he can seem innocent, remorseful, or earnest to please us, but this emotion is seldom sincere. He actually is lying to us and to himself. If we become fed up and ignore him, the sanguine will live more and more in unreality. It doesn't help to scold or get angry.

What is needed is to find areas where he can experience being at the center without hurting others. Encourage him to join a theater group where being in the limelight is not only acceptable but necessary. Or to join a sports team. On the sports field, the sanguine can have moments of glory by scoring a goal or making a good pass – but only by working together with others. He also finds that he must practice to stay in the team. Enjoying the limelight gives impetus to persevering with the hard work.

In both cases, the sanguine's initial interest will weaken, especially if concentration and energy are needed to make a breakthrough. He'd rather go on to something else. If you can enthuse him to try again, he begins to focus his will and overcome his superficial tendencies. A person who can inspire the sanguine to stay with it becomes much loved by him because this coach or director is addressing the sanguine's deepest yearning. Often sanguines will go through a stage, usually in the beginning of an experience, when they think they know more than the person in charge. They become moody when told to do something that they don't like and they threaten to quit because it's no fun to be there. But if they come to see that the other person was really correct and that they would have missed a wonderful opportunity, then they appreciate the other person. This is a turning point into the second stage.

Stage two

The stage two sanguine is full of good intentions but still lacks strength of character to follow through. No longer are these good intentions only for himself. Now the sanguine is trying to help others. He starts out with great joy, but when he meets obstacles, he's tempted to think only about himself. When he overcomes this temptation and stays focused on the other person, he has begun to transform his sanguinity. Then his gestures of interest in the other person become sincere and real.

Anecdote: Paula

For example, Paula was very difficult at home and at school. She couldn't concentrate on anything for long. She lost everything and couldn't remember things from one moment to the next. Her moodiness affected everyone around her. When her grandmother, who had Alzheimer's Disease, was brought home to live with Paula's family, one relative remarked, 'Great! Now we'll have two dingbats in the house.'

What came to pass, however, was quite the opposite. Paula developed a wonderful relationship with her granny. Her gentleness and understanding made her the person most able to cope with granny's constant confusion. The more helpful Paula was, the more she felt responsible for her grandmother. She was very proud of her grandmother's small achievements, and her cheeriness helped the other members of the household keep going in times of despair.

The key is for the sanguine to look up to another person with respect. (Often their heroes are cholerics.) Having chosen his 'hero', the sanguine feels happy to surrender himself (as long as he receives occasional strokes of recognition). He absorbs the achievements and recognition of his heroes and becomes selfless in emulating them. If the hero mistreats him or doesn't recognize him, however, the sanguine loses respect for the hero. That is the end of his devotion, and he lets other people know how much his hero has failed him. In doing this, he is even capable of resorting to viciousness and lies.

As the sanguine gains experience (long after those with other temperaments), changes occur. When he realizes how much he needs focus and depth, he consciously seeks people with those qualities. He's still a sanguine, however, and experiences a tension which makes him restless. He must test his 'mentor' to see if the mentor really is worthy. Often this consists of finding the mentor's weaknesses and insulting him. Many relationships end at this point. However, if the chosen mentor is mature enough, he or she will ignore this nonsense and get on with life. When the sanguine realizes that the mentor is not turned away by such unkind and silly behavior, he must reassess his behavior. This causes him to reflect, to go inward. When the sanguine can feel remorse for his behavior, a very important step has been taken.

Anecdote: Fred

Fred, a charming sanguine, had always made a good impression. As a child, he was the most loving of all his siblings. He was the one who ran up to his aunt and uncle, threw his arms around them, and told them how much he loved them. His warmth was delightful. In school, he had brilliant ideas, loved discussions, and enjoyed being with his friends. He had trouble finishing assignments on time, often staying up all night to get them in. But he did get them in.

Later, working in his career, he impressed people and he did well. Then he made a surprising career change. Instead of continuing to be the 'golden boy' in a field where he could rely on his ability to get along with people, he applied for a job that required skillful organization, meeting deadlines, and supplying information to others. His work was valuable only if it helped the other people in his organization. When questioned about this choice, he replied, 'I needed to take on this challenge and see if I could handle it. It represents everything I've had trouble with and didn't like.' The positive side of his sanguine temperament helped him see all kinds of possibilities to make the job more interesting and more fun, and he made good progress in his job and in developing his personality.

In a marriage, the sanguine temperament can bring great joy or great challenges. The optimism and enjoyment of life can make each day together a new adventure. The sanguine can lighten up a spouse whose temperament is melancholic, phlegmatic, or choleric – or he can try the patience of and infuriate the spouse. Much depends on the spouse's temperament. Two sanguines can feed each other's weaknesses and live totally self-serving, exciting lives, trailing the damage behind them. If they are balanced sanguines, however, they can be responsible – if a bit chaotic – and give each other hope just when it's needed. Their ability to see the bright side and always to try again brings strength to their relationship.

A sanguine who is immature can strain the marriage with flirtations, even affairs. A phlegmatic spouse may have the most patience to deal with this. If the phlegmatic wife feels secure, she will not take the escapades seriously, because she knows in her heart that her husband does not really mean anything by it. She has to love him deeply to accept the situation. If she is able to put up with his nonsense, she may find that he unselfconsciously tells her what he has done. He will not make excuses or deceive her. He is devoted to her, but he has his problem. She becomes the anchor of his life. A phlegmatic husband may respond similarly to a flirtatious wife. The important aspect here is that the sanguine desperately needs an anchor and will be devoted to the person who serves this function, at the same time as he or she does everything to destroy the connection. One day, the phlegmatic spouse may have had enough and leave. Then the sanguine is confused and can't understand why his spouse has left just when she's most needed. The sanguine husband or wife who behaves in this way is very much at risk. Very few people will put up with this kind of behavior, and it is hard to say that they should.

Instead of expressing itself in love affairs, this sanguine obsessive-ness may show up in alcohol or drug abuse, but the dynamic is the same. The sanguine in that situation is like a helpless child unable to control his behavior. If a person (spouse or friend) to whom he is devoted insists on a change, this can help focus the sanguine. The sanguine wants to be loved; threatened with the loss of that love, he will become desperate. From this low point, the sanguine may begin to get a grip, because the other person shows the way

Because sanguines resent efforts to change them, chastizing them does not help. What they need is patience and support for their good qualities. Ask a sanguine to do tasks that can be completed quickly and which have variety. If you question whether he can finish it, he will be proud to show that he has succeeded. As he completes one task, he builds strength to tackle another and follows it through. If a task is too monotonous or needs a lot of time, however, he will grow discouraged and become annoyed with you (not with himself). As sanguines grow stronger and stronger and are able to focus their positive, loving qualities on doing things for others, they can enter the third stage.

Stage three

One of the deepest experiences for a sanguine comes when something traumatic happens – a death in the family, a serious illness, a very serious problem in a relationship – something that cannot be ignored. Then the sanguine is confronted, cannot escape, and must focus. It is as if the sanguine has finally landed on the ground. This experience drives sanguine personalities inside themselves for a time and has a sobering effect for years to come. This will leave the sanguine not only with an intuitive feeling for other people but with real experience to go with it. Such experiences of grief and sorrow mature the sanguine and help him develop a new relationship to the world.

A sanguine's home and lifestyle may be chaotic, but he can also be light and amusing. Small problems don't get in the way. It doesn't matter if the dishwasher is broken and the water is leaking. The sanguine hardly notices. 'Oh, is it? I hadn't noticed.' There are so many things to do in a day. The sanguine rushes in and out of the house, drops things on a table or bed, and is out again. It is not surprising that the sanguine's car runs out of gas or that he doesn't notice that there's no more milk in the refrigerator. But it can be great fun to visit a sanguine's home. Things are scattered here and there. We can put our feet up and be comfortable. There's laughter, joking, and general good will. Unless we happen to ask for a book that we lent him six months ago.

'Book? What book? It must be here someplace. Oh, dear! I didn't get to read it. There have been so many things to do.'

There may be a guinea pig in a cage in one corner of the living room, a fishtank in another, a shell collection, stamps, and knitting in a jumble, but the sanguine is off to deliver meals to elderly people or to write letters for hospital patients.

Anecdotes: Charlotte, Brenda

Charlotte is another sanguine. Disorganized and scattered, she loses important documents and drives everyone around her into a dither looking for them. But she has high ideals and is devoted to her work with an organization which helps handicapped children. She enjoys meeting people and telephoning them with invitations to tea. Her friendliness and ability to make people feel comfortable encourages them to contribute to her organization. She sets deadlines for projects, but she is always in a rush to complete what was due yesterday.

She creates emergencies for the people she works with. They have learned to appreciate her work despite this frenetic style. Now, when she calls and says, 'I must have this tomorrow,' they quietly say, 'It will be ready next Monday. It's such an important project that I must do it well.'

She bargains, 'How about the day after tomorrow?'

'No, next Monday.'

Finally she accepts it and gets on with her work. It wouldn't help for the other to say, 'Look! The last time I hurried a piece of work for you, you lost it!' or 'The last time I stayed up all night to finish my section of the project, you weren't ready with yours.' Such comments only antagonize the sanguine, who already has a difficult time organizing himself. Firmness and enthusiasm work best. Charlotte is sincere in her efforts, but she just can't organize herself well. Nonetheless, her results are excellent, and she enjoys the praise that is showered on her and forgets the heartaches.

Brenda was a very sanguine teenager. She could finish nothing she started. She fluctuated between saying how stupid she was and how much she hated the adults around her who were demanding things of her. She threw fits, haughtily snapped her head up into the air, and threatened to run away and kill herself. Outwardly, she was impossibly arrogant, but inwardly she was crying for someone to help her take hold. The big step for her came when she joined the volleyball team. Neither her friends nor family expected her to stick with it. Because of this, her parents were reluctant to spend money getting her a uniform and shoes. Indeed, she did walk off the court a number of times. She did threaten to quit. She did abuse her coach in a terrible way. He ignored this and called her up in the evening and told her that he wanted her on the court the next day. He needed her. The drama that went on between them was fascinating. She did everything to make him lose confidence in her. However, he took her on as a challenge to his patience. By the end of the season, not only had she become a very acceptable player, but she adored the coach. And she had gained the confidence that she was a worthwhile person who could achieve something through hard work.

This confidence carried over into her academic work. Naturally, she had times where she wavered and relapsed. 'Oh, I knew everything so I didn't have to study. But I hate that teacher because I didn't get a good grade.' However, with the ups and downs, Brenda was clearly making the transition to the second stage.

In stage three, the sanguine's charm and sweetness are softened, and the sanguine becomes a lovable, generous person. He applies his intuition and experience to understanding people. He is the great helper who will be at your side just when you need him. He no longer scatters his ideas for attention, but puts them out for anyone to take and develop further. He no longer needs the recognition. His optimism keeps him young and gives him the forces to encourage others to try again. At this stage, the sanguine enjoys doing things for others for the sheer enjoyment and is almost embarrassed at their appreciation. It is difficult to believe that this is the same person whom we met earlier, in the first stage. A sixty-eight-year-old sanguine woman told me, 'Every day, I find something very small to be grateful for. Then I feel, '"This has been a good day!"' '

Stage three sanguines continue to enjoy sociability, but now they are less scattered. They take pleasure in bringing people together, listening to conversation, and observing new relationships that are forming. They are accepting of young people and their shenanigans, and often are quite permissive. Although the young people may misuse their freedom, they love these cheerful adults and come to trust them.

Sanguine is the typical temperament of childhood. When we think of what it is to be a child – lighthearted, changeable, joyful – then we have a picture of the sanguine. Just as the brooding of middle age typifies the melancholic temperament, and the equanimity of old age typifies the phlegmatic temperament, so the carefree nature of childhood offers us a picture of the typical sanguine. When the sanguine temperament is a strong ingredient alongside any of the other temperaments, it lightens and makes the other temperament more flexible, giving it more of a childlike gesture.

Chapter 5. The Choleric Temperament: Don't take so long. Just get it done!

Cholerics are solidly built, firm, and muscular. Their bodies are compact, ready for action. They are strong and give the appearance of being larger than they are. They often have broad shoulders, short necks, and strong chests. Their eyes have a strong, steady gaze with a touch of superiority. Their look of determination is at times misread as anger. Their facial expression and the way they hold their heads high show confidence, but also strain.

They speak with strong, loud voices and a commanding and confident tone. They take control of their bodies, often exercising vigorously. Although they are not as agile as sanguines, their bodies are strong and tough and can endure hardship. Boundless energy gives them a sense of being in charge. Although cholerics are well coordinated, they are not particularly graceful and may bump into people or knock things over.

The whole impression of the choleric is one of purpose. Her gestures are short and assertive with a forward thrust. Her heels pound the floor as she walks. Although she seems anchored to the ground, she is also restless. When she sits too long, tension builds in her body and she has to get up and move. She often paces while thinking. Beneath this tension there is a smouldering, her blood races, ready to boil up in response to threat or attack.

When a choleric awakens in the morning, she does not think of the day as another adventure as a sanguine would, but as an opportunity to accomplish something. Not easily distracted, she has her list and intends to complete it. Her sense of self is tied up with what she does. If she is at stage one, she sees the day as another opportunity to prove herself in battle, but if she has reached stage two, she sees the day as an opportunity to improve herself. At this stage, she sees life as work, rather than as competition.

Stage one

Socially, stage one cholerics are competitive. They expect to be first, best, biggest. Life is a contest and they are the deserving winners because they are the most capable. It is not difficult to see why others are intimidated by them. They are reliable, they have the energy to carry out plans, they know the best way it should be done – they are the masters. The choleric is glad to volunteer for a task, because she knows that the others are not as capable. She may complain about taking on too many responsibilities, but she wouldn't have it any other way. She delights in overcoming obstacles, and, with confidence in her intelligence, she will tackle almost anything.

Unlike the melancholic, who lives in the past, or the phlegmatic and sanguine, who live in the present, the choleric lives in the future. They set records and break them. Every minute is a new tomorrow.

When the choleric tackles a project, it is like a 50-ton tank moving into position. How she actually does the project will depend on how her choleric characteristics are influenced by the other temperaments in her makeup. For example, if she also has a strong sanguine quality, she will set about getting the work done without much discussion. Too much talk bothers such people. They just need to get started and they can fix things up along the way – knock down a board here, cut around a piece there! There's nothing they can't handle. But when someone suggests that they don't have the right material or equipment and says they should wait, they can't. They are itching to begin.

If a person's sanguine aspect is stronger than the choleric, she will probably take on too many tasks and have to call on her choleric drive to complete them. If she is a melancholic choleric, however, she will pay close attention to detail because the project must be done correctly. Once a plan is made and equipment organized, she brings her full energy to it and doesn't stop until it is finished. She will also check up on the work which others have done and reorganize it or redo it 'properly' if necessary.

When a choleric is working with another choleric, much depends on what stage they are in. If both are in the egoistic stage, the task quickly becomes a competition. They constantly look over to see how much the other has done. There is an unspoken race going on. At other times, they wager over who will be first or best or who will do the most. They may become loud, argumentative, and aggressive, taking comments personally and holding grudges. Two kings are trying to occupy one throne.

The choleric has something to say about everything. If she is listened to, all is right with the world, but if not, she pouts. Luckily, this passes quickly unless her honor has been attacked. In that case, look out! She can be vicious. She can easily see the other person as a representative of evil, challenging her, the representative of good.

When others stand in the way of her ideas, the choleric becomes bossy and pushy. She moves into a position of authority, either because another person steps back, or because no one else will take on the task, or simply because she belongs in charge. Once she has made up her mind, she is not easily influenced. She stands her ground and won't give in. Strong words won't dissuade her, and punishment won't work. What is most effective are soft words from someone whom she respects.

Anecdotes: Irma, Hilda

Irma is a pleasant, no-nonsense woman. She mothers everyone around her. Up early, she launches her plan for the day. Storming into the kitchen, she puffs and grunts as she prepares a large breakfast, cleans pots and pans, all with much clattering and determination. Then she bellows, 'Breakfast is here. I'm off to the garden. Clean up after yourselves.' She's not upset, she just has lots to do. She's a woman of purpose. In this way, she goes through her day, doing one job after another.

Her friend, Hilda, also a choleric but with a strong sanguine aspect, has much to do as well. When Hilda comes into the kitchen to make breakfast, however, she doesn't attack it as Irma does. Nonetheless, Hilda is cooking, reading, finishing a letter, and folding laundry – all at once. She relishes not wasting a minute and prides herself on getting it all done. It doesn't upset her if the tasks aren't done perfectly. After all, look at all she's accomplished! Irma would not be satisfied unless each job were done thoroughly, but for

Hilda, it is different. She is not so much the general of an army as the mayor of a village, which she must organize.

Anecdote: Muriel

When she was a child, Muriel visited her aunt – a choleric-phlegmatic – and uncle. When her aunt put dinner on the table, Muriel complained that she didn't like it.

'Fine. Just sit there until you eat it,' her aunt calmly said and went about her business, showing neither pity or anger. 'In my house, you eat what's put in front of you.'

Muriel couldn't impress her aunt with stubbornness. For several hours she sat, while everyone else in the household ignored her. Muriel was holding out – but for what? After what she thought was enough time to show them that she really meant it, she ate the food, which by then was cold. She didn't complain about the food again. And when she returned to her own home, she didn't complain either.

Cholerics are fighters for humanity, lovers of freedom. They are smart, have stern self-discipline, and consistency. They keep their word and aim high. If they must sacrifice themselves to accomplish their goals, they are willing to do so. They organize strategy, bark out orders, and stay with the task to the end. If they are fighting for a moral cause, they will not sell out. They have so many ideas that they are quite willing to share them – as long as they get the credit. They are not interested in money so much as in power. Their secret wish is to be recognized as indispensable.

Anecdote: Sam

Sam teaches history at a small college. He is a small, wiry man with a sweet disposition, but his choleric temperament dominates most of the time. There are very few colleagues whom he respects. When a faculty committee discusses plans for reorganizing the departments, he knows what has to be done. He can't stand it if he has missed a meeting in which decisions were made, because they are bound to be the wrong decisions. When he explains his position (which he delivers like a shotgun blast) and others don't agree with him, he is convinced that it is because they have missed his point. So he explains again, even louder and more strongly. It is impossible for him to grasp that his colleagues understood him perfectly well but didn't agree with him. He grows exasperated, his voice breaks, and he ends up stomping from the room. The next day, he is apologetic. He is sweet and gentle – but can't help trying one more time to explain his position. When the few colleagues whom he respects talk with him later, he sheepishly says, 'I know – but if they'd only listen to me.'

It is difficult for a choleric to accept criticism and blame. A choleric who thinks about the situation and sees that she is really at fault will try to sort it out. This will not happen in the heat of the action, but in the quiet afterward. It is painful for a choleric to realize that she has done something wrong or harmful. In her heart of hearts, she wants to be appreciated and respected by other people. When she sees that she is at fault, she eventually will apologize, but only if *she* decides to.

Anecdote: Rita

Sixteen-year-old Rita was at home by herself. Her grandfather, whom she dearly loved, stopped by and commented that the place looked a mess. 'Your mother isn't much of a housekeeper! Do you think you could help her?' he said gently. He hadn't directly criticized her, so her honor was still pure. When he left, Rita became a whirlwind. She took everything out of the kitchen cabinets and filled the sink with hot, soapy water. She cleaned every dish, organized the cabinets, washed the stove, scrubbed the floor, and had the place shining. When her mother returned, however, Rita stormed, 'No one cleans up around here! I had to do it all!' If she hadn't loved her grandfather, she wouldn't have done it. Because she respected him and he had asked for her help, she had poured her energy into it.

The next day, Rita went to visit her grandmother. As she walked in the door, her grandmother noticed that Rita's jacket had a ripped pocket.

'Why don't you fix it?'

Rita's face turned red and she flew into a rage. 'You always criticize me! You never see anything wrong with my cousins, but you are always picking on me. This has been going on for years!' By that time, she was sobbing. 'I can't stand the way you do that.'

One might think that Rita was being melancholic, but no! The choleric can't stand criticism and reacts out of her temperament. Depending on how she felt about her grandmother, she would either sew the pocket to please her, or refuse to sew it just to assert her independence. It is difficult for the choleric to be objective and simply see a torn pocket as something to be sewn. Instead, the critic becomes a rival, and a battle of wills takes place.

Young cholerics may contradict or resist their employers, becoming hot-headed and stubborn. Unable to accept criticism, they are seen as arrogant and land in trouble. It is not surprising when cholerics lose their jobs. Too often, they tax the patience and good will of their employers.

Anecdote: Ellen

Some cholerics may rein themselves in at school or at work but are tyrants at home. At school, Ellen was a delightful sixth-grader. She loved learning, respected her teachers, and cooperated. At home, however, she was a tryrant. When her sister didn't do what she wanted, Ellen hit her. When she didn't get what she wanted, she threw herself to the floor and pounded it. When her parents punished her, she wouldn't give in and show that she was sorry. Stubbornly she pretended that punishment didn't touch her.

She would show them! She would make them feel sorry that they had challenged her, so she crawled under her bed and said that she'd stay there all night. At mealtime, Ellen's phlegmatic mother became concerned that Ellen would miss dinner and begged her to come out. Ellen lay there, filled with satisfaction; her mother was feeling remorse for what she had done. But Ellen wouldn't give in.

'No, I don't want to eat your awful food.'

Her mother put the plate on the bed. Ellen refused to come out, but as the hours passed, she reached up and took the plate with its cold food. 'I'll show them! I won't eat it when it's warm.' She cleaned off the plate, all the time feeling satisfaction that she had won. Some hours later, she crept out and climbed into her bed with the sense that she had won a battle. She had given them no satisfaction.

Stage two

In order to move into the second stage, a choleric must undergo several changes. First, she must learn to adjust to other people and situations. She must see that there are times when she cannot be in charge. When a choleric realizes that she is not going to be given the leading position just because of who she is, this is a big step. If she continues to see herself as all-important and superior, she gets stuck. Second, she needs to listen to other people's experiences. If she can see others as having worthwhile skills and be able to respect this, that is an important change of perception. ('But,' the choleric will add, 'that person better be worth his salt!')

The choleric wants respect and admiration. If she sees that her behavior arouses contempt in those around her, she feels terrible. People whom cholerics respect need to stand up to them and call them on their behavior, but not in an aggressive way. When confronted without rancor, the choleric will abandon her egoism and no longer attempt to force her will on others. She yearns to be met as an equal by those who are fearless and in control of themselves. Then her egoism is left powerless and her attitude turns cooperative.

Anecdote: Victor

Victor was taking advantage of his position at work. He knew that he was working very hard and was needed, but finances were tough and he decided to take on a second job which would involve using the equipment at work. He didn't think that he needed to ask anyone's permission. He was putting in so much extra time on his job! How could they refuse him? It was owed him. However, other employees grew very annoyed about this. He was monopolizing the copy machine when they needed it for their work. One of the older managers, himself a matured choleric whom Victor admired, called him in. 'I'd like to talk to you as a friend. This extra work you're doing during the day is causing a few problems. It's nothing terribly serious, but some of your co-workers who respect you so much are questioning it. They like you too much to criticize you. But maybe you can think about it.' This was exactly the right way to approach Victor.

Victor thought about it and brought it up at the next staff meeting. He explained what he wanted to do. He said that he was spending many hours at home on his primary job, and that occasionally he needed to use office equipment for this second job. He fully expected to pay for whatever supplies he was using, and he would be happy to stop using the equipment when other workers need it. He said that he was open to suggestions and comments and that he hoped the situation could be worked out with their cooperation. It was. Victor retained the respect of his co-workers and made a big step in considering the needs and feelings of others.

Cholerics want to be unique, to be themselves. When they are part of a group, they stand out as leaders. As they move into stage two, they realize that they depend upon their fellows for recognition and admiration. If they are not recognized, they work even harder to do better. They cannot rest until they know that they are appreciated.

Of course, a choleric may relapse to stage one, especially when she meets new people who seem weak. Then the choleric will dominate them and ignore their views, at least until the newcomers assert themselves.

Is the choleric cold and hard?

No! Her goodness of heart is not immediately apparent for two reasons. First, she is so focused on completing her task that she may appear cold. Second, cholerics often antagonize others with their pushiness and feel that they must protect themselves against real and imagined attacks. They cover their sensitivity and softness with gruffness. With tact and kind words, we can help the choleric feel comfortable enough to show her softer side.

When faced by other people feeling sorry for themselves, the choleric becomes impatient and unsympathetic. Why does this person keep whining? Why doesn't that person take hold of life and stop complaining? The choleric tires of hearing people complain about situations in which they feel helpless. Such weakness deserves no respect! However, real sorrow moves her profoundly. She can be extremely generous if she experiences a real need.

We can help the choleric by appealing to her sense of chivalry, which is hidden beneath a forbidding exterior. By assuming that she possesses this quality, we force her to live up to our (and her own) expectations. Magnanimity and generosity are two virtues of cholerics, but they need to be evoked. This can be done by showing that we know that those qualities exist. This approach is also effective with a choleric child.

Anecdote: Christina

When I worked in a home for emotionally disturbed children, we had an extremely choleric child, Christina. When she was even mildly chastised, she ran to her room. With tremendous strength, she picked up her bedsprings and threw them against the wall. During dinner, if another child said something that Christina didn't like, her face would puff up. She would push her chair back from the table, stomp to the door, and slam it so that the walls shook. What worked best was to say very calmly, 'Christina, would you please close the door again. I know that you can control yourself.'

Again, she would slam it.

Again, we would calmly speak our request.

Again, she would slam it.

This went on several more times. After a while, however, she grew exhausted and would close the door quietly and sit down.

Then we would very calmly say, 'I knew you could control yourself. Sit down and finish your dinner now.' The explosive tension had subsided into calm. She would feel better for several days.

A choleric woman has a particularly hard time. She longs to find a man as strong as she is, but she often scares such men away. Strong men are often looking for a less domineering, more feminine woman. Although they may enjoy working on a team with a choleric woman, they don't necessarily want to marry one. Her self-confidence, high standards and critical quality makes life a competition. She is constantly demanding and is seldom satisfied. She is longing for a man who can stand up to her, who is calm where she is a storm, to be wise where she is clever, and to be strong where she is testy.

In fits of rage, the choleric may destroy what she has taken years to build, insulting and bullying in personal relationships, breaking walls, ripping her favorite paintings, throwing her beloved tools into the trash.

The mood in a stage one choleric's house may be tense. Choleric parents may be shouting, with children arguing back or cowering with fear. Criticism is harshly doled out. On the other hand, some choleric households are balanced and cheerful – where the cholerics plan all kinds of excursions – backpacking, mountain-climbing, rafting. They delight in life's challenges. They get things done. Whether they've decided to redo the garden or remodel a room, with bantering and loud talking, there's activity going on. When the choleric parent maintains balance, his or her blunt comments and criticism can be felt as love and concern.

Stage three

When the choleric develops respect for the personalities of her fellows, we know that she is approaching Stage three. This is very difficult for her to do. Cholerics have plenty of courage, including the recklesness of youth, but the courage needed for this significant change is different. As long as she can blame others for failure, she doesn't make changes. The most important moment for her comes when she realizes that the fault lies in herself – that she is not infallible. At that point, she may give up altogether, withdrawing into herself, blaming herself for everything. Her knees weaken, she feels a chill go through her, her courage ebbs away. Realizing that she is not as powerful, as self-sacrificing, and as effective as she had thought, she begins to question herelf. For some cholerics, this marks the awakening of a religious life.

At that moment, the choleric needs the greatest understanding from her friends. Criticizing her only stirs up the old anger. She has already judged herself more harshly than anyone else can do.

How can we help her? We must challenge her to use her gifts. We know that with her intelligence and skill, she can work it through. She will be worthy of all that she admires in life if she can now transform herself. This is the kind of selflessness which she has really been seeking as an ideal. All along, she has been wanting to serve humanity in the way she thought best. In this moment she realizes that it was the way that was wrong, not the goal. She must demand of herself the kind of effort that she has been demanding of others. First, however, she must learn to control herself and recognize her own faults and shortcomings. She must realize that the way to perfection is by painful, laborious effort. To be fit to lead others, she first must learn, through experience, to lead and discipline herself.

Anecdote: Janet

Janet went through a very difficult divorce. She was able to take control of everything else in her life, but she was helpless in the face of the pain of her divorce. An acquaintance who had known her for several years commented to her, 'You are accessible now. You used to give the impression that you had all the answers, but this pain you have gone through has softened you. Now you are not so intimidating.'

Although cholerics are natural leaders, they have a two-fold task if they are to progress in their development. On one hand, they must develop compassion, generosity, and forgiveness toward those around them. On the other hand, they need to become objective about themselves and accept responsibility for their actions. This is the development towards stage three. This is a formidable task for the choleric who must overcome so many of her earlier temperament traits. Many are unable to change and remain ambitious people locked in a struggle for power. Our political life is filled with such people. When cholerics do accomplish this transformation, however, their strength can contribute positively to society.

When the choleric, through self-knowledge and self-discipline, reaches stage three, she is able to let go. She still may feel an occasional desire to step in and set things right, but she holds back. Now she provides support and confidence to others, and when she asks how things are going, it is out of interest, not out of a desire to control.

Stage three cholerics keep an eye out for younger people with outstanding qualities and encourage them. Younger people turn to them as mentors and advisors. They become fatherly or motherly friends who are respected and trusted. They appreciate this admiration, but they no longer demand it or need it.

Until they achieve this third stage, cholerics are often avoided because of their brusqueness and argumentative style. They achieve exactly the opposite of what they really want, namely, appreciation and respect. Instead, they engender fear and a feeling of suffocation. It hurts them so deeply to hear that, and they can't understand why. They give everything to their job, working long hours. They bring so much experience to their responsibilities, and they want to do only what is right. Whatever they do, however, they somehow cannot dispel this feeling of resentment. A person who wants to come close to a choleric friends or boss needs to show sincere appreciation and admiration. (If it is insincere, the choleric will sense it.) Once the choleric respects him or her, generosity and sweetness may pour forth. If an employee or friend is having a hard time but is able to admit his mistakes, the choleric will reach out with forgiveness. Deep in their hearts, cholerics are generous people, waiting for opportunities to give. They often cover up these feelings because they don't want to appear weak, but they are grateful when a situation allows them to show their finer qualities.

How can we help the cholerics? Avoiding them doesn't help. We must understand where the choleric is drawing her motivation. She does not think that she is working out of a need for power but out of a need to contribute. When she criticizes, she does so because she honestly sees failure in other people's work and she wants to improve the situation. Others need to realize that the choleric's criticism is a demand for perfection.

In her interaction with others, the choleric needs to learn to control herself and to see into the minds of others. If she cannot gain this self-control she becomes desperate and only sees herself surrounded by incompetence and laziness. But the mature choleric has much to offer, and it is well worth helping her develop.

If we ignore the choleric or constantly block her, she feels trapped and must break out. Then we see the worst of the choleric temperament: stubbornness for its own sake, power games, and destruction of other people.

Anecdote: Tristan

Tristan is director of a small firm which he has built up, and he knows that without him it would be nothing. When he travels on business, he calls the office constantly, making sure that all the tasks he left behind are being done. His staff is happy for some breathing room while he is gone, but they know that the minute he steps through the door, he will have them all trembling with fear. They do their jobs and get everything done. They marvel how easy and calm the office is without him. They do even more than he asked.

When Tristan returns, his booming voice is heard first. He's in a jolly mood. 'How are you?' he says to each one he passes. He doesn't stop to hear their answers, but moves around his kingdom, checking the pulse. Everything seems fine, but did they not miss him when he was gone? He must tell them all that he did.

'Yes, I have a wonderful surprise. I met the owner of a hardware firm on the airplane and I sold a large account to him. Yes, I did. It's a fine day.'

The office workers look at each other. He's in a wonderful mood, but they know that 'the moment' is coming.

Then he calls his staff into the office. 'Now what has been done? What? You didn't do the whole mailing list? Why not? Didn't I tell you that it absolutely must be done?' He doesn't listen for the answer. By then, the employees are shaking. He doesn't listen long enough to find out that they have made sensible judgments.

'This is what happens when I leave town! My staff is not competent to run things without me.' The fact that the secretary used her own initiative and slightly changed his order was too much. By the end of the day, both he and the staff are exhausted from his bombastic responses. He is convinced that he must not leave town again, while his staff can hardly wait until he does.

Then one day, his meek secretary asks to talk to him. She has been thinking about this for months, but each time she lost courage at the last minute. She makes sure that there is time, that he knows that it is something very important to her, something that will help her. She explains that she is having a problem. She is very loyal to the firm. She admires her employer very much and feels honored to work for him. She considers this one of the best firms in town and she can learn much from his imaginative vision and ability. He is listening because she has told him how important this is to her. She has been a faithful employee. Then she tells him that she finds it very hard to deal with his explosions. She explains that he always tells his employees to use their initiative, but when they do, he blames them for mistakes. She explains that when he starts yelling, her stomach knots up and she can't work properly, that she becomes less efficient. Does he think that he could show them how to best use their initiative so they can strengthen their skills and take more responsibility?

Her employer Tristan looks at her with new eyes. She's not such a weak little mouse. This young lady has some strength. She handles herself well. His heart warms. 'I know I'm rather blustery at times. I'm sorry if I hurt you. Yes, yes – of course, I can help you out. Let me think about it.'

She leaves, pleased that he has listened to her. She hopes that he will follow up on his promise, but, most of all, she is pleased by her courage to face him. He wasn't so bad after all. He has quite a nice side.

About a year later, Tristan announces that he has taken on a partner, Peter. He is a wonderful person, full of enthusiasm and good ideas. Everything goes well for two years, and then fireworks begin. Tristan doesn't approve of some of Peter's ideas. Peter's work isn't as thorough as it should be. Some clients prefer Peter to Tristan. All these observations begin to boil up in Tristan. In the middle of an argument, Tristan suggests that Peter leave. It isn't working. Peter is not what Tristan thought he would be. For a few weeks it seems as if Tristan will leave. There is chaos.

A wise mutual friend becomes aware of the crisis and speaks to both men. 'Your partnership isn't going to work if this tension continues. We must have a conversation.' Respected as a fair person by both Tristan and Peter, the friend meets with each man and lists their grievances. Then he meets with them together. Although Tristan tries to explain away each of Peter's grievances, the old friend is calm but persistent.

'I know this sounds harsh, but I think there's something to this,' he says. 'Why don't you take this list home and think about it? Let's meet again tomorrow.'

At home, Tristan storms and fumes. He shouts at his wife. He denies that he behaves like this. As he thinks more about it, after he has made a dozen excuses, it dawns on him that maybe he does behave in this way some of the time. He is horribly embarrassed. He had thought that he was acting only for the good of the firm. Maybe this is what his secretary had been referring to. From somewhere deep within he begins to feel, 'I must put this right.'

He feels that he's failed his mission. He goes into temporary melancholy. He can hardly face himself. By the time he meets with the old friend the next day, he is eager to admit that there is truth in Peter's complaints. Gradually there is a reconciliation, although Peter still decides to leave the firm.

Tristan is moving into stage two. When he listened to his secretary, he was beginning to show respect for someone else. When he began to see his behavior and feel remorse for it, he was moving away from egoism, toward objectivity.

Tristan continues in his development although he has his moments of relapse. But he has wise employees who value his contribution, even though they find his egoism unpleasant.

Over the next few years, he identifies a successor and mentors him. When Tristan retires, he will be busier than ever, but he won't be responsible for the office or under pressure of keeping the business moving. It is his experience that will be helpful. Meanwhile, he has been thinking about the situation with Peter. He gives it a great deal of thought and watches his behavior very carefully. He really wants to be a kind-hearted person, but he feels heavy responsibility to make the firm successful. Tristan recognizes that he is mellowing. His wife feels it too. People are more attracted to him now. He is asked to serve on several boards. He is a fine person, with much to offer. Tristan has moved into stage three.

Cholerics make a powerful impact on their surroundings. They impose their will on others, they make things happen either by pushing ahead before others are ready, or by taking initiative when no one else does. They are the movers and shakers. It is to everyone's benefit when cholerics learn to balance their power with thoughtfulness.

Chapter 6. Through the Windows of the Temperament to Individuality: Spinning Straw into Gold

We all know people who have strongly one-sided temperaments. What is it like to be a melancholic, a phlegmatic, a sanguine, or a choleric? Since each of us has all four temperaments within us, we should be able to identify occasions when each of the temperaments has arisen in us. Here are some examples.

Name the temperament!

It is a rainy Saturday. I don't have anything scheduled, so I decide to clean out the closets. There is no hurry. I take everything out and give the closet a good dusting. Now I rearrange the shelves, putting nice new paper on them. I organize my shoes and place them in boxes. Then I put my skirts together, blouses together, jackets together. I take time to look each one over for tears or spots to be cleaned.

The hours go by. When I look at my watch, I realize that the whole afternoon has gone by, but that's OK. It feels good not to be racing the clock. It feels good to discover that my jacket needs cleaning when I have time to do something about it instead of when I go to put it on. Instead of throwing my things into the closet to get them out of sight, I am taking time to put them away properly. I feel relaxed. It is good to be putting order into my life again. I am really enjoying myself.

Now, I sit and have a cup of tea and relax. So this is what it must feel like to be a phlegmatic! So there is some phlegmatic in me, after all!

The morning begins as usual. The alarm goes off, I shower, dress and eat breakfast. When I go to the car, a tire is flat. The pump is not in its usual place. It is growing late. Finally, I find the pump and pump the tire up. As I drive onto the highway, traffic is backed up because of an accident. I inch past the accident scene and glance over at the ambulance and the wreck. Oh, dear! I hope it isn't anyone I know! It looks as if no one could have survived. I begin to feel anxious. What if my husband has been in an accident?

Finally, I arrive at work. On my desk is a note saying that the report which I handed in yesterday needs to be revised, that it contains too many errors. I start worrying about whether I may lose my job. How terrible that would be! What would I do? By noon, I can see that it is going to be one of those days I'd like to forget.

The day continues in that manner. My father's neighbor calls to say that my father has been taken to the hospital for observation – possibly a stroke – and I must go there after work. I start thinking about my widowed father – what will happen if he is paralyzed? Will he come to live with us? That would mean rearranging part of the house. We would have to hire help. Where would the money come from? As I begin my work, I feel anxiety creeping in. I start worrying. My head aches, my shoulders ache. Am I getting sick too?

The phone rings. It's a message from my friend's secretary, canceling dinner tonight. I want to tell my friend all that is happening – how awful I feel, how worried I am about my father – but the secretary has delivered the message and hung up. I can't do anything right. So the day goes. On such a day, I can feel the anxiety which a melancholic carries around all the time. We all have troubles and difficulties, and we all have a melancholic tendency to feel overwhelmed by them, but usually we can put them aside and get on with our lives. That is what is so difficult for the melancholic, who continues to feel miserable, even after the trouble is resolved or disappears.

Life has been very routine lately. Why don't we do something different, something exciting and out of the ordinary? Let's be extravagant and go into the city. Let's do whatever strikes our fancy – no plans, no worries about money, forget our responsibilities. We quickly dress and get ready. Savoring our adventure, we are about to step out the door when the phone rings. It is my brother-in-law, reminding me it is our turn to mow the lawn at my parents' home and to do whatever chores are needed around the house.

'No, I'm not going.'

'How irresponsible!' he says. 'We agreed we would alternate Saturdays.'

I have been regularly putting in my Saturdays for the last three years, so his accusation grabs – but I don't let it throw me. We're having an adventure today and no chores are going to stop us! Off we go, and we have a wonderful day. We pay a surprise visit to a friend, we do some shopping, we pop in at the art museum. Everything seems new and fresh. Exhausted but happy, we return home, feeling years younger. Why don't we do this more often?

Today we have been sanguines. This is the way a sanguine approaches every day. When someone tries to remind the sanguine about responsibility, he brushes it off as boring and tedious. He won't let anyone spoil his fun.

The smell of smoke wakes me up. Where was it coming from? The kitchen, the baby's room? As I realize that we are in danger, I can feel my adrenaline surge.

I jump from bed, immediately thinking about the children. I must get them out! I have an amazing rush of energy. There is nothing I can't do. As smoke fills the house, I run into the baby's room, grab her, and quickly move to her brother's room. Three years old, he is still sleeping. I snatch him up and now, with both children in my arms, I rush into the living room. The door is locked. My blood is racing. Frantically, I put my son down, unlock the door, grab him, and kick the door shut behind me. We are outside and the children are safe!

I run next door and the neighbors call the Fire Department. By then, the children are crying. We cover them with a warm blanket and give them something to drink. Meanwhile, I am thinking of how to reach my husband, of who our insurance agent is, of where the important documents are, of the baby's medicine. All these things race through my mind. With clarity. I jot them down to give to the firemen when they arrive.

Later, I wondered how I could be so much more in control of a situation than ever before.

That is the choleric in me! That is how the choleric feels much of the time. There is no time to waste. Important things must be done despite obstacles. We must act! Whether it is a physical danger such as a fire or a decision about changing the logo of the company, there is always something very important involved – and no time to waste.

Once we gain empathy for someone else's strong temperament, perhaps we can find a way to be helpful or at least understanding. The more we work with these images, the more we can see our own actions clearly. Understanding our temperaments is not merely one of life's curiosities. It enables us to recognize how great an influence temperament in its various stages exerts in our lives. Because children are so impressionable, the temperaments of their parents and teachers have a strong influence. Because I am a teacher, I am especially interested in the effect of the teacher's temperaments on children.

In its egoistic stage, any temperament can be destructive.

Temperament in the Classroom

The melancholic teacher

The melancholic adult is a terrible burden for children while the mature melancholic adult is a blessing. The melancholic demands sympathy, pity, and understanding. Surrounded by the fears and anxiety of the teacher, the child will also grow anxious about the world. Children learn to tiptoe around and not disturb the melancholic parent or teacher who doesn't feel well, who doesn't like loud noises, who doesn't like the curtains parted to let in the light. When a teacher throws away a child's work because the eraser made a smudge, the children become nervous about bringing their work up to show to the teacher. They aren't sure that their work is very good. What if it ends up in the wastepaper basket? They don't feel very worthwhile.

A melancholic teacher may nag, whine, and threaten to call the parents. Some melancholic teachers have even threatened to put an end to themselves if the children didn't behave. When I was in seventh grade, a teacher told the class, 'If you don't stop making that awful hissing sound, I'll jump out the window!' The rascally seventh graders hissed louder.

When parents come to speak to a melancholic teacher, they may never get to make their point. The teacher spends the entire conference telling them all his personal problems and difficulties. They may feel pity, but the parents leave the room confused and wondering why that person is even teaching. The teacher, having unloaded his worries, feels better.

Yet a mature melancholic is a wonderful teacher. Filled with sensitivity and insight, this teacher has a particular soft spot for those shy children who shrink into the corner. The teacher's gentle manner, interest in the children's work, and love of nature and beauty all radiate into the classroom. Occasionally, louder children are difficult for this teacher to handle, but his love for animals catches their interest and soon they are helping feed the turtle or the hamsters. The children are quiet because there is no need to be loud. Parents seek out this teacher as a listening ear who will sympathetically hear their problems and, when asked, gently offer advice. The children develop delicacy in their drawing, a love of detail in their writing, and sympathy for each other. The teacher fosters a special caring for those who are in need, and the class may collect clothing for earthquake victims, make regular visits to a convalescent home, or make beautiful cards for friends who are sick.

The phlegmatic teacher

The classroom of the immature phlegmatic has quite a different mood. Instead of nervousness, there will be either lethargy or tumult. Phlegmatic teachers in stage one may care about the children but are too focused on themselves to notice things. They don't make demands, they are uninvolved, they don't want to be bothered. Children may be chasing each other around the room, but the teacher doesn't even notice. The room may be stuffy because the teacher didn't notice that the windows were still closed. In a methodical and boring fashion, children and teacher go through their lessons. Nothing is very interesting, voices are monotone, life is dull, dull, dull. The children feel suffocated.

A mature phlegmatic, however, is a natural teacher. Unflapped by the sanguinity of the children, the teacher is steady and thorough. His good nature helps the children feel secure. This teacher has time to help, time to read an extra story, time to sit with the class on a rainy day and enjoy a special treat. The children feel their teacher's peacefulness. They are able to finish one task before they begin another. They may not finish all that was planned, but what they do, they do well. If the teacher promises to do something with the children, it is done. The children can depend on their teacher to be fair and to do what is promised. Children from other classes like to come in, because the classroom is peaceful and cosy. Children's work is organized beautifully, with nice cubbyholes and lovely little name tags. Chores are done by the children because they enjoy the order of the room.

The sanguine teacher

The mood is very different in the room next door with its sanguine teacher. Immature sanguine teachers make everyone nervous by fluttering around, never finishing a sentence, misplacing lesson plan books.

When work is handed in, the teacher exclaims, 'Oh, how wonderful!' – without noticing that the child's work is upside down. Four or five projects are going on at once. Supplies are a mess, glue bottles sit without covers, brushes are unwashed, pencils are scattered. On the other hand, there is lots of activity and scurrying around. Excitement is in the air. Eventually, however, unfulfilled promises, trips that don't happen, and lost projects accumulate, building resentment in the children. The teacher gives an assignment, but changes instructions several times, confusing everyone. Just as the children settle down to their work, the teacher tells them it's time to go to the next subject. The teacher starts telling a story but is distracted by a fly and loses his train of thought. The story goes on and on, in this way and that. It is all exciting, but what happened to the main character? The teacher is charming with parents and promises them whatever they want. When the parents realize that it is all talk, however, they feel manipulated. Several parents gather together to try to bring some order. They organize the next class trip and make sure that there is enough food for all the meals.

The mature sanguine teacher, however, is a delight for everyone. Full of enthusiasm and interest in the world, the teacher makes life joyful. He awakens wonder in the natural world, teaching the children how beautiful and special are the animals, the plants, the stones. Learning is an adventure. The children sweep in on the waves of the teacher's enthusiasm as they write stories, draw pictures, make up plays, and compose music – developing all their talents as they explore their studies. Individual children are given special assignments to deepen their particular interests. The room may not be as well taken care of as the phlegmatic's room and desks may be a little chaotic, but the children are learning – and they love school.

The choleric teacher

Choleric teachers in stage one can usually be heard before we enter the room. Their voices boom as they shout commands. They bully the weaker children who can't stand up to them. They argue with the cholerics, who are challenging them. It feels as if a fight will break out any minute – and this would happen, except that the teacher threatens the children with a terrible punishment if they misbehave, and they know he'll carry it out!

When a child asks a question, the teacher may take it as a personal challenge, an insinuation that the teacher doesn't know the subject. Children with other views than the teacher's won't raise their hands. There is only one right answer. If the teacher makes a mistake, he cannot bear to lose face and will make up some lame excuse. Driven to anger, an immature choleric teacher will resort to pinching, slapping, pushing. The children feel resentment, anger, and fear.

I sat in one such room in which the teacher kept bullying the children. When a child stepped out of line, the teacher pushed him back in. The teacher insulted the children, called them names, and incessantly shouted. As I sat there, I felt that even I needed a shield to protect myself, and I'm sure the children did too. Stomach aches and headaches were common.

Parents don't have a chance with the immature choleric teacher. Convinced that he is right, he doesn't listen to parents. Instead, he criticizes, threatens, and so overwhelms the parents that they either refuse to approach him any more or they take their complaints to a higher authority. Parents often fear that the teacher will retaliate against the children if the complainant is identified.

The mature choleric teacher, by contrast, makes a strong leader for children. He learns to try the impossible and to succeed. He finds his strengths and focuses on them. He can paint the room, haul stones to build a wall, and work with perseverance on spelling. He makes charts to see who learns their multiplication tables first, but also shouts with joy when the last child completes them. He is directed, firm, and supportive. The mature choleric is impressed by the great heroes of literature and history, and is devoted to being brave and kind and fair. He inspires others to identify with the doers in history as they celebrate freedom, victory, and triumph. The mature choleric is aware of his tendency to monopolize and makes an extra effort to listen.

None of us is either entirely immature or mature. Mostly, we live in between, at the second stage, where we have good days and bad ones. Moreover, we rarely express only one strong temperament. Nonetheless, these pictures bear enough truth for us to find ourselves in them and to see how it must be for those around us. The variety of temperaments in a school or in a family makes life interesting and balanced. We cannot be everything to our students or children. That is why we need each other. Our colleagues and our spouses who experience life so differently bring other possibilities into the children's lives. The more we learn to understand the temperaments, the more we realize how important it is to take hold of and transform our own, and the more we appreciate those around us. We can also learn how best to support our colleagues or spouses so that they can develop a more balanced approach to life.

Temperaments in the Workplace

In our workplaces, our temperaments play a strong role in shaping the way we handle responsibilities and relate to our co-workers, employers, or employees. The better we understand this role, the better we can carry out our tasks and the more fulfilling our work will be.

The melancholic in the workplace

Melancholics like to work alone with a specific task. They need time to think. If a task is divided into small steps, the melancholic isn't so overwhelmed. From time to time, gently remind him of the deadline. Ask the melancholic for help with your task; you'll be surprised how willing he is. But be careful about putting an immature, one-sided melancholic in charge of an office. He will either worry all the time or spend too much time telling people his troubles. On the other hand, the mature melancholic may be sensitive enough to see where he needs help and is able to reach out for it.

For the mature melancholic boss, having a jovial phlegmatic or sanguine secretary or assistant can bring a good balance, as long as there is mutual understanding and appreciation. The mature melancholic is a wonderful listener, bringing perspective and thoughtfulness to personal relations as well as to the tasks on hand. His challenge is to develop courage to express his opinions and not be intimidated by others. Constantly struggling with whether he is worthy or not, he needs to experience his ideas being discussed and even rejected, without feeling that he himself is being rejected.

The phlegmatic in the workplace

Phlegmatics like routine work that gives them time to think. Therefore it is helpful to assign one task at a time without rushing them. They need to have all their supplies organized in compartments. They will do detailed work carefully and slowly without mistake. Supervisors need to check on their work casually, from time to time, giving praise and then showing the next step.

They are reliable and will carry out what the supervisor requests as long as directions and expectations are clearly understood.

Phlegmatics tend to keep to themselves, but they don't mind being around people from time to time (as long as the others don't start poking around or moving things on the phlegmatics' desks or shelves).

Occasionally, the supervisor should show the phlegmatic a new way of doing something that has been successfully tried elsewhere. Lay it out step by step. Otherwise, he will keep using the old trusted methods and materials. Be careful about asking a phlegmatic to make too many decisions under pressure of time. Given enough time, however, his carefulness and thoroughness contribute important points of view to decision-making.

One also should exercise caution when it comes to putting phlegmatics in charge of other workers. Either they have trouble making decisions and confronting those who aren't doing their jobs, or they come across as charging elephants. If they are mature phlegmatics, however, or if their melancholic qualities are balanced by either choleric or sanguine qualities, they can be very effective managers or leaders. Their challenge is to develop interest in other people.

The sanguine in the workplace

Sanguines love company and prefer to work where they can talk to someone. They may talk so much that they distract others from their work while accomplishing little themselves. Be very specific about what has to be done and about deadlines or they will do a little bit on many different tasks. Because they tend to be disorganized, it's prudent to make copies of important documents in case they lose the ones you give them. Give lots of small tasks that can be finished easily. Keep doing this until the sanguine asks for a bigger job.

A sanguine in charge of an office or department can have special challenges. His disorganization can create chaos. If he is a mature sanguine, however, and especially if he has a reliable staff, the sanguine can be a creative, exciting leader. His staff can make sure that the meetings happen on time, that letters are answered, that documents are filed, that visitors who have been casually invited are received properly, and so on. It is the sanguine's ability to meet people, to sense new directions, to initiate projects, and to inspire others that creates new possibilities. His challenge is to strengthen his will power, to follow through and to focus.

The choleric in the workplace

Next come the cholerics. If they are not already in charge, give them plenty of challenges – jobs that no one else can do. Be very clear about the line of command or else they will take over. Show appreciation for what they do. Let them know exactly what they must do to advance in their jobs. Don't get upset when they tell you how to do your own job; they are just trying to be helpful. Don't overreact when you hear that they've been rude or pushy to other workers. Calmly mention it to them and ask them to bring you a solution the next day.

The choleric makes a good organizer or leader, but he needs people around whom he respects, to keep him in line. He may be able to do this by himself if he has come to understand his impact on others. His challenge is in working with groups which are trying to come to consensus. The choleric needs to restrain himself, to be patient, to leave space for shyer or more contemplative colleagues to speak, and to listen. He knows that the fire in his soul can warm or it can burn, so he tries to be aware of this. His challenge is to develop patience and respect for others.

How to help?

One way to help a melancholic is to arouse his sympathy by telling him your problems. Let him tell you his, as well. Ask him questions about himself, his family, his work. Keep asking questions, not staying too long on any one. Ask for help, and make it a direct request. Don't expect him to pick up hints that you need help. If we show understanding to melancholics, we are rewarded by their confidence and by their stepping out of their shell.

With phlegmatics we must be gentle and not confront them. Stress the sensibleness of what you want to do. Stress quality, practicality, and durability of whatever it is you want to buy or make. Give them time.

With sanguines, encourage them to pursue their interests. Praise them when things are done well. Be careful about boundaries. Don't let the sanguine manipulate you, and call him on it if he does. Find legitimate ways for him to shine.

Appreciate cholerics. Don't assume that because they are so strong they don't need praise. When going to a choleric for advice, tell him that you are speaking to several people and that you expect to learn something from each. That way, he won't expect you to do everything he recommends nor will he feel that he will be responsible for your decision.

Helping ourselves

By working with our own temperaments, we can bring equilibrium to our personalities. In each temperament are virtues which would moderate and balance the extremes of our dominant temperament while still allowing us to express our individuality. To achieve that balance, we need to consciously cultivate the positive qualities of those other temperaments which live in us but do not dominate. Often, one temperament dominates during childhood and another in adulthood.

Cultivating the objectivity of the phlegmatic can help lift us out of our anxieties. Cultivating a sanguine lightness can help us get out of our doldrums, enabling us to feel hope. Cultivating a choleric courage can help us plan for the future, and cultivating the melancholic's concern for others can make us more sensitive.

Phlegmatic?

If we are chiefly phlegmatic, we may make a special point of showing interest in the people around us, asking them about themselves, seeing how we can make them more comfortable. We can set ourselves the task of learning a new skill to crack ourselves loose from the confining shell of our habits – something different from what we are doing now, to draw out the sanguine side of ourselves.

Becoming concerned about other people, learning about their problems, and finding the capacity in ourselves to relate to them awakens the melancholic in us and helps overcome our phlegmatic tendency to indifference. At the same time, modeling ourselves after some cholerics whom we admire can help us bring more energy and drama into our relationships.

Melancholic?

Those of us who are mainly melancholic need to learn a thing or two from the cholerics, about asserting ourselves positively and getting to grips with life, moving on into the future rather than looking back on the past. We can also learn from the sanguines that things don't always have to be taken quite so seriously, that we can 'lighten up' a bit; and from the phlegmatics that we don't have to carry the burden of the whole world on our shoulders, for 'what will be will be'.

Sanguine?

Those of us who are predominantly sanguine can work on concentration exercises to strengthen our will. We can choose a cause which we admire and volunteer our help, making sure to be there regularly and on time. We need to gain more focus and command of ourselves. These are choleric qualities that can help us manage our sanguine tendency to flightiness. While the sanguine is already quick to help others, cultivating his melancholic side can develop a deeper, more enduring concern and sensitivity. Cultivating phlegmatic qualities may mean that the sanguine makes his life more rhythmical – waking up, going to sleep, having meals at regular times.

Choleric?

The cholerics among us need to strengthen their appreciation of other people's skills and talents. That may mean taking a cue from the melancholics: taking time to listen to other people's needs; taking a cue from the phlegmatics: slowing down and becoming methodical; and taking a cue from the sanguines, not taking ourselves so seriously and being able to laugh at ourselves.

Another way to look at our temperamental traits is to look at the three soul forces of thinking, feeling, and willing. Each temperament is associated with particular qualities, allowing us to develop ourselves positively.

Thinking

When we examine the qualities of our thinking, we can be grateful for the melancholic's contemplative side, depth, and love of detail; for the phlegmatic's objectivity and thoroughness; for the sanguine's flexibility and optimism; and for the choleric's ability to focus on the ideal and create a broad picture. If we were able to develop all these capacities in ourselves, we would have balanced thinking.

Feeling

In our feeling life, if we were to have the melancholic's kindness, thoughtfulness, considerateness, and appreciativeness; the phlegmatic's good nature and even temper; the sanguine's hope and joy; and the choleric's sense of responsibility, we would have the capacity to cherish beauty in nature and in art, and to bring harmony to our human relationships.

Will

If we could cultivate in our will the melancholic's gentleness, the phlegmatic's patience and steadfastness, the sanguine's love of variety, flexibility, generosity, and adventure, and the cholerics's perseverence, sense of responsibility, and courage to aim for the stars and to set goals, we would have tremendous capacities for doing good in the world.

Although few people start out with such balance, we can cultivate these qualities. The balance of temperamental qualities enables us to achieve the highest development of our individual expression. We also can experience such a balance, however, when we work together in groups where individuals contribute these diverse aspects. When we accept and appreciate each other, the decisions we make can become the reflection of a greater and higher unity to which we all make our individual contribution.

It may be tempting to pigeon-hole people simply in terms of their temperaments, but we must always resist that temptation. The temperament is only one window through which we can see the human soul. It is one tool, and it can be helpful as long as we don't think it is the only way. Let us also remember that the temperaments themselves are not static, fixed, limiting conditions, but rather are starting points with infinite potential for the development of the individual's full humanity. Our task is to see through the temperament, not to look at the temperament. Our object is to see in the other human being a worthwhile individual who is a spiritual being just as we are, who has needs and cares, ideals and struggles. In other words, our object is to perceive the human spirit.

SECTION II

THE SEVEN SOUL QUALITIES AND THE JOURNEY THROUGH LIFE

Soul Qualities

When the child reaches puberty, her soul life frees itself from her physical body and she experiences it as a separate entity. Something is waking up. She feels herself to be in a different relationship with the world. The temperament which had dominated her personality no longer acts so strongly. Instead, the soul life awakens, so that she yearns to unite her individual inner world with the outside world.

This aspect of the human being Rudolf Steiner calls the astral body. It is not a body in the way that we can refer to the physical body, but more a body of forces that carries both the lower and the higher soul life. For example, it is because the human being has an astral body that she develops desire. Once the astral body has totally penetrated the physical body, the child is sexually mature. Previously the child had desires, but they were of a different kind. 'I want that cookie', 'I want to have that toy.' At puberty the astral body penetrates the entire physical body including the sexual organs. Pubic hair develops. The girl's breasts develop. With this new activity of the astral body, sexual desires awaken. Another aspect of the newly awakened astral body is the change that occurs in thinking. The child is able to form clearer concepts. She takes in the world differently. We could describe it pictorially as a 'breathing in' of the world.

The adolescent's newly freed soul life or astral body has a broad range of responses. At first she is concerned with what is closest at hand, such as her feelings of belonging in her family, her group of friends, her school. She is concerned with everyday issues – what to wear, whether to talk to a friend who spoke behind her back, how to apply for a weekend job, whether or not to audition for the school play or basketball team, whether or not to go to a party, whether she in love with her boyfriend.

As her soul life expands she relates herself to the wider world and engages in broader issues – how to solve pollution problems, is cloning moral, how to care for AIDS babies, does there have to be poverty, is there is a God, what is the nature of Truth, what does Love mean, and what is the purpose of my life? She carries her feeling of love outside herself and wants to share that love with others. She not only wants to understand what is happening to her, but she wants to understand others.

Edna St. Vincent Millay expressed the expansion of the soul life so well in her poem 'Renascence'.[1]

> The world stands out on either side,
> No wider than the heart is wide.
> Above the world is stretched the sky
> No higher than the soul is high.
>
> The heart can push the sea and land
> Farther apart on either hand.
> The soul can split the sky in two
> And let the face of God shine through.

Another element of the newly awakened astral body is the development of reason and judgment. The young adolescent tends to judge situations by imitating her parents or her friends. She may agree and voice her agreement without much thought behind it, or she may take the opposite point of view just to show her independence. In later adolescence, she is able to judge out of herself, even if she has to stand alone. Her astral body and 'I' are working together, and she is able to make judgments based on her true values. The ability to reason object-ively grows stronger every day, and therefore the adolescent is able to engage in schoolwork through conceptual thinking, to enter into abstract thoughts, understand assumptions, prove theorems, analyze a character's development in a novel, and apply such reason to her own life.

With the awakening of the astral body, the young person expresses a new relationship to the world through idealism, through hopes and dreams of what she will do or become. Over time she develops a more objective relationship to the world and adjusts her idealism to reality. Without the idealism of the adolescent, human life would be dreary and limited. Adolescent idealism transforms sexual desire in the form of the crush. Holding the hero or heroine on a pedestal can give the adolescent time to mature before engaging in deep romantic, sexual relationships. Adolescent idealism expands a young person's thoughts and feelings beyond everyday life. Which one of us would have wanted to do away with the hopes and dreams that arose during our adolescence? They inspired us to dream the unimaginable, attempt the impossible,and awaken to the possibility of spiritual existence.

The adolescent expresses this new relationhip through seven soul attitudes. Each soul attitude shows itself in the way she relates to her individual inner world and to the outer world. There are several ways psychologists have formulated to identify types of people – for example by using Enneagrams, the Myers-Briggs personality scale, or by identifying people as introverts and extroverts. Rudolf Steiner pointed to seven different types, often referred to as the planetary attitudes, soul types, or soul attitudes. These are the ones I will describe in this section of **Soul Weaving.**

Since the soul is the carrier of the forces of thinking, feeling, and willing, the soul types express particular qualities of thought, feeling, and willing as they express themselves in the astral body. Each person has all seven personality types in her astral body. Some soul types are more strongly connected with feelings, others with will, and others with thinking. Some people may express one particular soul type throughout life, others may express other soul types at different stages of life.The soul attitudes continue to express our relationship between our inner world and the outer world for the rest of our lives.

The soul types or soul attitudes are different from the temperament. The temperament is more strongly influenced by a person's physical body. A heavy, slow-moving person tends to be phlegmatic, whereas a thin, wirey, fast moving person tends to be sanguine. The temperament continues to influence us even after the soul attitude begins to express itself. For example, a person may have a strongly inward-directed soul attitude as a 'Spiritual Investigator',[2] but her temperament may still be sanguine. At first this may seem unlikely, but let us imagine someone who has a wide variety of interests. She may be a deeply thoughtful type, focused on her inner thought life, but her temperament pulls her in many directions. This may express itself in a roomful of clutter, a frustration at not being able to give full attention to each interest. On the other hand, the Spiritual Investigator may have a choleric temperament. This person would have the inner fire and strength to finish projects, to pursue research despite all kinds of obstacles. If the Spiritual Investigator had a melancholic temperament, she might close herself off from other people and take refuge in her inner life completely. When she encountered obstacles, she might give up, figuring bad things always happen to her. She is more likely to feel the heavy burden of life. The Spiritual Investigator who has a phlegmatic temperament would tend to *be very methodical in her research, to focus on her inner thought world and take each obstacle as it comes without getting overly distracted by it.*

*The temperament is more difficult to change because it is so much of a habit. We **can** transform our temperament, but it takes very strong action on the part of our 'I'. Because of this we are far less in control of our temperament than of our soul attitude.*

Chapter 1. The Seven Soul Qualities

The next step in human development occurs during adolescence with the emergence of the soul type. There are seven soul qualities or soul types which begin to express themselves during this stage and which continue into adult life. As the young person relates her inner life to the outer world, a characteristic 'gesture' develops. Some people live more strongly in their inner world (introverts), others in the outer world (extroverts). Some actively engage in life; others are relatively passive. The individual's soul quality is influenced by the combination of introverted, extoverted, active, and passive tendencies. Out of this interaction, positive gestures can develop as well as negative ones. The work of the 'I' is to transform negative aspects so that the soul qualities can express themselves in their most positive way and provide a constructive force in human relationships. As we make decisions out of our dominant soul quality, we are at the same time forming and defining our character.

Each of us bears elements of every soul quality, but usually we express one or two more strongly. And at different phases of our lives, one or another of the soul qualities manifests more strongly than at other times. These qualities exert a softening or hardening influence on our dominant soul type.

I have used compound names for the soul types to try to get closer to the various qualities expressed by each one (see Appendix for notes on the sources of these names).

Six of the seven soul types can be more clearly understood when described in pairs. The seventh is an integration of all six.

The extroverts

In the first pair we have two soul types both of which define themselves in terms of their relationship to the outer world. Both are extroverts:

Active Talkers are involved in the world. They are creative and purposeful, filled with strength and energy to make things happen. They consciously want to change the world, to make their mark. Through their words and deeds, things are accomplished.

Dreamy Nurturers passively allow the outer world to work on them. They react to outer circumstance when it intrudes upon them, but their first priority is the emotional life. They are concerned with the needs of others and express this through compassion. They bring love and beauty to life. Yet they can be taken advantage of, and can drift off into a world of illusions.

The introverts

In the second pair, we have soul types which are best understood in terms of their relationship to the inner world. Both are introverts:

Spiritual Investigators actively pursue the inner life, searching for truth, trying to bring spiritual considerations into everyday life. Because their 'I' is very strong, they are focused on the self. This tends to make them self-conscious.

Reflective Preservers focus on the inner life in a passive way, swayed by impressions. They remember what happened in the past and use the past as their guide. Reflective Preservers need routine and tradition and don't actually like change. They can be scholarly (as with the intellectual dreamer who forms abstract concepts) or artistic (as with the dreamy, moody artist). Their 'I' is often too weak to stand up against the outer world.

The balancers

The third pair is neither extroverted nor introverted. Their relationship to inner and outer worlds is one of balance:

Thinker Organizers see the Big Picture. They look at life objectively and make plans and structures to hold it all together. They experience the world in the present, think about it, and bring it into balance. These people are in command of the situation, but in a quiet way. They don't lead aggressively, but calmly, out of inner authority. They strive to bring order out of chaos.

Social Innovators keep things moving, bringing people together, healing through flexibility and humor. They adapt and adjust easily to the outer world. There is a constant flow between inner and outer. They, too, live in the present, moving between one person and another, maintaining connections, and looking for opportunities to bring about something new. They may create chaos as a way to make something new happen or just because they want excitement.

Radiant Balancers are the seventh type, which stands by itself. The defining quality of Radiant Balancer is harmony and equilibrium. Very few have such a high level of balance in their soul lives. Each of us has some of this quality within us, shining through our souls and helping to bring healing wisdom, love, and joy. Through the influence of the Radiant Balancer, the 'I' is able to draw the best out of the other soul qualities.

Soul qualities during the life stages

According to Rudolf Steiner, each stage of life comes under the influence of a particular soul quality. This is based on his research into planetary forces (see appendix).

> Birth to seven: Reflective Preserver influence.
> Seven to fourteen: Social Innovator influence.
> Fourteen to twenty-one: Dreamy Nurturer influence.

Twenty-one to twenty-eight: Radiant Balancer influence.
Twenty-eight to thirty five: Radiant Balancer influence.
Thirty-five to forty-two: Radiant Balancer influence.
Forty-two to forty-nine: Active Talker influence.
Forty-nine to fifty-six: Thinker Organizer influence.
Fifty-six to sixty three: Spiritual Investigator influence.

After sixty-three, we experience the influence of all the soul types and are more free either to work with them or ignore them.

Soul qualities in everyday life

Picture a community meeting in which neighbors have come together to discuss building a playground for the children. They straggle into the living room where the meeting is being held. One neighbor has arrived early to make sure the room is cozy and inviting. Chairs are placed in a circle. A flower arrangement is on the table. The aroma of percolating coffee greets the arriving neighbors. Then someone comes in and right away starts talking about the project.

'Let's get going. We don't have a long time to talk about this. The children need a decent place to play. We can start digging Saturday morning. I'll bring shovels. You bring rakes and hoes. We can finish in two days if we all work steadily.'

Another says, 'Wait a minute. Has there ever been a playground in that spot? We have to check with the county to see what regulations are binding. Which children are going to play there? Are we talking about a playground for toddlers or for nine- and ten-year-olds? What about an area for skateboards?'

One neighbor waits patiently and then says, 'Look, I brought some large sheets of paper. Let's draw the plan. We have to have an idea of what the whole playground will look like. We can't just start without an overview.'

The neighbor who has come in early and wants to start on Saturday morning grows agitated.

'You're going to talk and talk about it and nothing will ever happen. I'm ready to work, but I don't want to sit while you dream up ideas.'

Tension builds. What seemed such a simple task is turning into a complicated process with various people taking strong positions which other neighbors have trouble understanding. One who has been silent all evening begins to speak. This person wants to discuss the idea from the beginning.

'Why are we doing this in the first place? Maybe the children would be better off playing in their own yards? We don't know that a playground will solve the problem. Let's get to the real issue? What's the relationship of a playground to a neighborhood? Does it enhance the quality of life, or will it just be a place to hang out?'

The conversation continues.

'I'm very anxious that we make a decision at this meeting. We have been talking for two hours.'

'Everyone knows that this is a very serious issue and will take much pondering.'

'I'm really upset. I thought that this would be such a nice way for us all to come together. Wouldn't you like a cup of coffee? Maybe you'll feel better if you have something to drink.'

'We haven't made a list of equipment for the playground. I think we should have the swings with rubber seats. Oh, yes, we need sand under the swings, so no one gets hurt.'

'Can't we make some decisions?'

'Look here, do we want a sandbox in this area, or is it too close to the climbing bars?'

'I once saw a wonderful playground with a corkscrew slide. Maybe I can find out where they got it.'

'When I was little, I used to climb up and go down such a slide over and over again.'

'Maybe we should put the playground on a rocket and shoot it into outer space. That would be a thrill.'

'Oh, it's so nice that we're getting together and meeting each other. I've been wishing we'd do this for a long time. Would you like another cup of coffee?'

One neighbor storms from the room. Another runs after, eager to patch things up.

Can you imagine such a meeting? Have you ever found yourself in the middle of such a situation? Perhaps you have begun to recognize some of the soul types.

Let's look at another example. Imagine a family scene. Grandmother has died and her grown children have gathered to plan her funeral.

'I'm so upset. I loved Granny so much! She was the heart of our family. What are we going to do without her?'

'Look, the florist is open only till noon. We have to make some decisions. Let's stop being so sentimental and get on with it.'

'What are you rushing for? We have three days until the funeral. Let's work this all out. How many people are we going to invite? Who's putting the notice in the paper?'

'Remember Grandmother loved pink. We should have pink hyacinths and pink satin lining in her coffin.'

'The issue here is not what we want! What does Grandmother really want – to be cremated or to be buried? This is a very serious issue. Let's deal with what would have real meaning for Grandmother.'

'Maybe we should dig the hole at night under the full moon!'

'Oh, stop making jokes! This is serious. Don't you have feelings about Granny?'

'Of course I do, but everyone's getting so serious and stuffy. I'm just trying to lighten things up.'

'Remember, whatever we do, we shouldn't have the funeral at 3pm. Grandmother always had tea at 3. Then she took her rest after that.'

'Are we going to decide something, for heaven's sake?'

When we are in the middle of such emotional scenes, it is difficult to step back and realize that *each person is bringing an important aspect,* one that needs to be considered. However, each can get stuck and see only one side of the situation. Such scenes occur every day and lead to bad feelings among neighbors and family members. If there is someone in the group who can appreciate the gifts of each and is able to keep the process moving, there can be cooperation, and the common task can be accomplished. The more we understand these soul types, the more we are able to see each other's sunny (and funny) side and help each of us reach balance. We need them all, yet each soul type can become an obstacle if it grows too one-sided – and then it can drive everyone else mad with frustration.

Chapter 2. The Active Talker

Active Talkers want to get things done – now! They are creative but purposeful. Whatever needs to be done should get done without wasting too much time. There's a lot that needs doing. They need challenging, difficult tasks. Impatient with the present, they are always focused on the future. What happens out there in the world is what matters. This means that some situations are handled abruptly and without grace. The Active Talkers are the leaders, the ones who get things done.

Active Talkers speak strongly and well and can communicate their purposes effectively. They know how to use words to put their point across. Their weakness is that they can use their power to persuade others to take a position against their better judgment. For example, Active Talkers in Congress or Parliament are good at 'twisting arms' to get votes for their cause. In these situations the words themselves may be less important than the forcefulness of their delivery.

They have many creative ideas, and they love to move things along, to see their ideas realized. As soon as one idea is realized, they have another.

Their energy is concentrated and focused. They keep moving, exhausting themselves. Their energy is so strong that they often build up and then break down what they have completed, because they need to keep doing.

When Active Talkers are too one-sided, they bump up against other people and engage in a battle of wills. Hot tempers lead them into situations where they may destroy a month's work in a rage. But difficulties or not, they like being pioneers and getting things done. They make good business people because they see life as a competition, love risks and like to prove themselves.

The Active Talker expresses himself in terms of power. When his power is too focused on overcoming others or exerting his might, he may destroy what stands in his way, whether it be a business competitor, a rival on the athletic field, a colleague, or family members who would use their own power to resolve conflict, confront evil, or protect weaker people.

When they are balanced, Active Talkers are inspiring leaders. Their challenge is to redirect their energies from confronting outer obstacles to inner ones, to allow their tenderness to evoke the best in others. Active Talkers have tender hearts, but other people often don't realize it. As they turn their focus inward, soften their hard edges, and develop gentleness, their positive thoughts come to the fore. Once they see their own weaknesses as problems to be solved, they apply themselves with great energy and earnestness to overcoming those weaknesses.

Cultivating an inner life is a particular challenge for Active Talkers, because this is where they tend to be lazy. They rationalize, putting aside their inner development by saying they have no time for it, that too much else needs to be done. They would rather talk than contemplate. They can do ten things at once in the outer world, but slowing down to look inward is difficult.

Active Talker as adolescents

Adolescents with Active Talker qualities are looking for action. They struggle with untamed energy which forces itself upon friends, siblings, classmates, teachers. They set up confrontations because they see others, especially those in authority, as rivals. They must prove to themselves and others that they are not cowards. Impatient with process, with contemplation, with details, they want to get to the point, get the action going. This impatience is also expressed in relation to their schoolwork. If a teacher asks an Active Talker to redo work, he becomes furious or dashes it off. Convinced that he knows better, he argues with his teachers about how his work is evaluated. In a rage, he may slam down books or throw a tantrum as he exits from the classroom, steam pouring from his ears. Many people – children and adults – are intimidated by this behavior and avoid confrontations.

Deep down, the Active Talker is looking for people whom he can look up to for their strength, for their ideals, for their ability to take on difficult challenges and overcome great odds. This doesn't mean, however, that he will roll over like a puppy in the face of a strong adult. Rather, he will test, annoy, badger, confront, argue with, and criticize the adult until that moment when he recognizes the adult as an equal. At that point, disdain gives way to respect. These young people will be loyal to such an adult and will improve their school work and behavior, because they yearn to be respected by their hero.

When adults react aggressively toward Active Talker teenagers, nothing is gained but a lot of tension and hot tempers. The adult has to keep calm and composed. This is true with Active Talker adults as well as with teenagers.

Many adolescents, and especially Active Talkers, are attracted by power. Whether it is to be better or stronger, they want to be on top. We can help them transform the negative aspects of this soul type by giving them challenges in which they have to use all their energy and courage to succeed and which benefit others. They want to be the leaders and until they get to be, they will criticize how things are done. But when they are given responsibility, they need all their energy to overcome obstacles. Through this effort, they gain patience, insight and appreciation for the efforts of others. Literary and historic accounts of great figures who overcome obstacles are inspiring for Active Talker adolescents. They yearn to do something important, something never done before. When their ideals are nurtured by these stories, they long to follow in their hero's footsteps.

Some gang leaders are Active Talkers who never had their ideals nurtured. They have not been given examples of courageous fighters for truth and justice, incentive to strive for righteousness, or reason to discipline their powerful energy. As they come into adulthood, Active Talker teenagers struggle to make their place in the world, to overcome obstacles, and to make things happen in the only way they know – by force. If, however, they can be inspired to transform their anger and feelings of helplessness into something positive, they can use their energy to help society. But much healing has to happen first.

Mature Active Talker adults

As Active Talker adults mature, their challenge is to transform their former behavior where it has been too one-sided. For example, if they have approached life as a battle, combating enemies, attacking, overpowering, bullying, impulsively reacting, or inflicting uncontrolled temper tantrums and bouts of anger on those around them, they have created serious obstacles for themselves.

Perhaps in his thirties an Active Talker will realize that this behavior was not in his best interest and did not satisfy his highest inner longing. He can take hold of this power and energy and transform it. When he directs power and energy positively, new capacities such as initiative, independence, moral courage, and self-reliance can develop.

The mature Active Talker understands the power of his words. He expresses his thoughts clearly and cogently without making them too strong. He holds back the force of his personality and offers his thoughts in a free way, so that others can accept or reject them on their merits. Rather than using words to sting and cause pain, the mature Active Talker brings warmth and concern into his speech.

Active Talkers transform their assertiveness by developing the ability to listen. By holding back their own speech and creating a space for others to express themselves, Active Talkers become sensitive listeners, able to recognize other people's ideas and capacities. Through this transformation, new social skills are developed. Learning to listen is a difficult process for Active Talkers, but it bears precious fruit when it is mastered.

The transformation of lower qualities into higher ones is not only a great achievement for the Active Talker but usually brings great blessings to society. As he strengthens his will for doing the Good, he is looked up to with admiration and respect. Because the Active Talker is such a powerful person, it makes a big difference whether transformation occurs or not. This soul type has the power not only to move mountains but to move large groups of people in either a positive or negative way (see appendix).

Chapter 3. The Dreamy Nurturer

Some people live strongly in their feelings. They reach out of themselves into the world to help, to listen, to make life nice for others. They pay attention to the environment, wanting to fill it with beauty and concerned that people feel comfortable. They like to create a space, to fix a room, and to create possibilities where things can happen. Then they sit back and watch. These are the people we will call the Dreamy Nurturers.

Rarely will Dreamy Nurturers demand center stage the way Active Talkers do. The Dreamy Nurturer exudes warmth, embracing others with her feelings. Like Venus, goddess of Love and Beauty, Dreamy Nurturers shower love on others. Their kindness evokes the best in the other person (see appendix).

Lacking a strong sense of time, a Dreamy Nurturer can sit for hours and listen to someone's problems. She can listen and listen and may have difficulty bringing the session to completion, because she is so concerned about the other person. Her receptive gesture attracts those who yearn to be cared for. Sometimes a Dreamy Nurturer goes so far as to forget about her own needs and loses her own sense of identity.

On the other hand, she can care too much for the other person and smother him or her. Intruding on the other person's space, she can create emotional dependency. Many people who enable others, who support the other person too much, are Dreamy Nurturers who are out of balance. They have good intentions, but they have difficulty respecting others' freedom.

Dreamy Nurturers often suffer because they want life to be pleasant, peaceful, and trouble-free – for everyone to be happy. But this is not always possible. They don't like being told, 'You can't please everyone' because that is precisely what they hope to do.

Dreamy Nurturers' strengths are often apparent only behind the scenes as they empathize with their colleagues or friends who have family problems, are ill, or have been passed over for promotion. If they are asked to carry major responsibility, they may not be able to do so effectively, because they become too easily distracted by other people's needs and lose sight of their own immediate goals.

If a friend is sick, the Dreamy Nurturer is in her element. She will care for her, doing everything to help the sick friend feel better. She will brew a pot of coffee or tea, fluff the pillows, and bring a bouquet of flowers. She has the best intentions and will volunteer to organize other friends to bring dinners over after a friend comes out of hospital, but it often takes an Active Talker or a Thinker Organizer to make it actually happen. The Dreamy Nurturer runs the risk of becoming too distracted while making phone calls to organize the effort, and instead spends several hours listening to someone else's troubles, never completing the whole list. Nevertheless, Dreamy Nurturers accomplish a great deal through their love for others.

Another aspect of the Dreamy Nurturer is passion. Undeveloped and one-sided, this passion can become a frenzy, sweeping her off her feet, causing her to lose sight of her goals, carrying her away so that she forgets what she is doing. Constantly needing to be in love, to have someone to care for, to lose herself in the passion of the moment, to seduce and to be seduced – these all typify the undeveloped Dreamy Nurturer.

The ideals and longings of the adult Dreamy Nurturer are those which are common to virtually all adolescents, regardless of soul-type, especially the quest for Truth, Beauty, and Goodness. When they do not find anything in life to satisfy these longings, their feelings of love can turn to hatred and become destructive. Such people develop fantasies in which they imagine doing terrible things to people who have disappointed them. Instead of opening themselves to the world, immature Dreamy Nurturer adults become narrow-minded and closed, over-sensitive and easily hurt.

An area in which the Dreamy Nurturer excels is the home. In past times, the Dreamy Nurturer woman had a central place in society, creating a warm and loving home, cultivating beauty in the home, caring for her children and husband. Today, these qualities are brought to bear in the workplace as well. Dreamy Nurturers make the rest of us more conscious of the need for an aesthetic work environment and of the value of supportive relationships or working conditions. Not only are people more productive in a nurturing environment, they are psychologically healthier.

A Dreamy Nurturer can become the 'earth mother' of her brood, or a martyr, exhausted by the demands of her responsibilities. If it all becomes too much, she may fantasize an escape from her burdens or seek refuge in her bed.

One Dreamy Nurturer spent hours organizing pictures on a wall so that they looked beautiful and balanced. She transformed the room so that it was welcoming and warm, with details that enhanced its beauty. She could sense what was needed and was willing to work slowly and quietly to realize it. By the end of the day, she was exhausted, but also satisfied that she had succeeded in making beauty live in what had been a dull space.

In our fast-paced life today, Dreamy Nurturers may have a difficult time finding outlets for their talents. They may drown in self-pity because they are not appreciated. However, when Dreamy Nurturers find occupations that acknowledge their inner longings, they become fulfilled adults. Interior design, poetry, writing, nursing, social work, and psychology are some of the areas that fit their needs.

In contemporary society, men who are Dreamy Nurturer types are more recognized and acknowledged than in the past. Such men may choose to stay home and nurture the children and care for the home while their wives go out to work.

It is not only artistic types who are Dreamy Nurturers. Some are intellectuals, who withdraw into the world of ideas, spin theories, and ponder life's big questions: Is there a God? What is the nature of Virtue? Of Truth? They love to discuss these topics. Some of the great philosophers as well as artists have the gesture of the Dreamy Nurturer. Meanwhile, they irritate those other soul types who want to see action, not mere dreams.

Dreamy Nurturers seek love and relationship, but in their desire to be loved, they can get themselves into situations in which they are taken advantage of or in which they mistake mere physical satisfaction for love. Such a person may search from partner to partner, looking for the perfect person. She may lose herself in flirtation and sexiness, burying her deeper ideals while she searches on the surface.

Many a Dreamy Nurturer goes through life looking for a silver lining but not finding it. She yearns for her youth, when she planned her life, spun her dreams. It hardly occurs to her that she is still dreaming, and that she needs to take hold and make some of her dreams happen. Dreamy Nurturers can be difficult in a group, because they have trouble coming down to earth and facing reality. At the same time, they bring beauty and loveliness into our lives, keeping alive the dreams and the ideals of our youth.

The Dreamy Nurturer as adolescent

It is during adolescence that capacities for love and freedom are born. Adolescents begin to develop their own identities, to experience independent, individualized feelings. Interest in love and sex develop. Adolescents are driven by a need to have intense feelings, to connect with members of the opposite sex, to share their feelings and thoughts. Sex is part of this, but not all.

During adolescence, love is the strongest impulse, not only love expressed in an intimate relationship but love for the world, for nature, for knowledge, for ideas, for all human beings. Working with Dreamy Nurturer adolescents is a special challenge for teachers because they do not usually have a bent for the sciences, mathematics or the facts of history. To pique their interest, the teacher has to find a way to connect the lesson with something tragic or beautiful that happens to a scientist, mathematician, or historical character. They can also be inspired by the beauty of number patterns. Once their feelings are engaged, they are more likely to find a connection with the subject. Otherwise, they show little inclination to get involved in anything remotely abstract.

Much also depends on how they feel about their teacher. They are not usually interested in learning for its own sake, so they need to feel a connection with the teacher. Perhaps the teacher has shared with them a love of poetry or some humorous experiences from her own adolescence or some past suffering. These are interesting to Dreamy Nurturer adolescents and may help them cope with learning what is otherwise not captivating for them. Often they like to escape into science fiction, romantic fiction, or other fantasy. They admire adults who love beauty and who appreciate love as a force in the world.

Dreamy Nurturer adolescents search for the good, the beautiful, and the true. If they are not inspired in this search, however, they grow cynical, and withdraw, often becoming self-centered and haughty. They escape into their inner world, their dream world, where they feel safe and fulfilled. If, on the other hand, their longing for the good, the beautiful, and the true is nurtured, they feel that life is full of meaning and joy, and their hearts are filled with gratitude and appreciation for all that people do for them, for the beauty of the world, for the glory of Creation. Out of this feeling arises a desire to give back to the world, to offer love and support for others out of their own sacrifice and pain. They carry the suffering of the homeless, of neglected children, of animals, of the neglect of the earth. When their feelings are stirred, they are moved to act. They will give away part of their allowance, go out and clean trails, serve meals to homeless people, care for wounded animals,or otherwise do their part in helping others.

How can we respond to Dreamy Nurturers?

Dreamy Nurturers need our time and attention. Their love for beauty and their caring for others often put them at a disadvantage with the more aggressive types, and the strengths of Dreamy Nurturers often go unappreciated by the world. These are qualitative traits which don't show up on tests and generally aren't acknowledged, either by the academic community or the commercial world. If adolescents can develop their talents, they gain strength and self-confidence. The great sadness for Dreamy Nurturers, especially in high school, is that they so often go unacknowledged. For a while, they may fight for recognition, but eventually they may give up and lose faith in themselves.

Teachers need to create opportunities for these young people to show their talents and contribute their artistic and social gifts to the group. Such projects as designing a cover for a theater program or brochure allow them to paint or draw or write for special occasions. Opportunies for them to express their compassion serve a useful end and elicit genuine admiration from peers. Dreamy Nurturers need a special niche in which they can show their authentic strengths.

A particularly helpful experience for Dreamy Nurturers is drama. In trying on different roles, they experience many sides to their own persona and have an opportunity to try them out. When adolescents experience love for the world during their teenage years, they can more easily experience brotherhood and caring for others when they become adults.

Mature Dreamy Nurturer adults

When Dreamy Nurturers bring their passion under control and permeate it with their 'I' they sort out superficial relationships from deeper ones. They become aware of their own needs and address them in a healthy way. On one hand, they yearn to be objective; on the other hand, they experience objectivity as cold, and they distrust it. Only when they become masters of their feelings and transform them, can they combine the warmth of their hearts with intimacy so that they are not taken advantage of. The mature Dreamy Nurturer must depend on her thinking to sort out her emotional life.

Dreamy Nurturers who have established balance develop an appropriate sense of giving to others and are still able to take care of themselves. They learn to select which demands to respond to, rather than exhausting themselves in trying to answer everyone's needs. Although at first they feel that they are being harsh, in time they recognize that their friends respect them for setting boundaries. Dreamy Nurturers spread joy, love and warmth. They bring wonderful gestures of friendliness and thoughtfulness. They are community people, meeting together, attending to celebrations and potlucks, bringing the extra special touch that brightens our day. Without Dreamy Nurturers, the world would be a cold and lonely place.

The gifts of the Dreamy Nurturers are evident. Their shining warmth elicits trust and sharing from their friends and companions, they radiate compassion and interest in others. We all need a good strong dose of Dreamy Nurturer soul quality to enhance our social relationships.

Chapter 4. The Spiritual Investigator

The Spiritual Investigator seems to look at the world from the farthest reaches of the Cosmos, all the way back to Creation. Gradually, he comes down to earth, but he always carries the memory of spiritual substance deep within his consciousness. Like the Greek god Kronos, the god of Time, the Spiritual Investigator is concerned with time and timelessness.

Spiritual Investigators live in their thinking. They are most at home in the world of concepts because they are always looking for the big picture. They focus inwardly in their active search for truth. They long to get at the real meaning of things. Much effort is made to probe every detail as they dig deeply and find the essence. People with this soul quality find it easy to be objective and unemotional. They are good researchers. They love libraries, books, and files. They ask such questions as, What was really meant? What is the truth? What were the real intentions? How did this all begin? What was the context? They need time to reach conclusions, because they take every situation seriously and want their conclusions to be right. They often have a clear sense of how an idea will work in the future, but may have difficulty communicating their perceptions so that others can hear them.

Spiritual Investigators approach the world methodically and slowly. When they are asked to make quick decisions, they are unable to respond and resent the intrusion. They have to ponder, to find the reasons. Before they can act, they have to know. Because they know how uncomfortable it is to be rushed, they also leave other people space and time to make decisions.

While some Spiritual Investigators can be tactless, others are very concerned about protocol. They hestitate to criticize; in fact, they don't like to get too close to another person's feelings. They are often reluctant to impose themselves on anyone and so they keep their thoughts to themselves. In the presence of more mercurial types, such as Social Innovators, they are horrified by the liberties these others take in asking personal questions. The Spiritual Investigator is happy to share his vision of what needs to be done but then he prefers to pursue the task methodically and on his own, without feedback from others.

Once they make a commitment or a connection, Spiritual Investigators are loyal, but if they are pushed too quickly, they can become spiteful and bitter. They tend to bring strong form to whatever they do. Sometimes this can become too rigid; at other times, it brings needed structure where there is chaos.

In social situations, Spiritual Investigators are often awkward. Consequently, they prefer to work in situations where they can be alone and concentrate on what needs to be done.

Without other soul qualities to enliven them, the Spiritual Investigator can become hardened and impervious to the outer world. He tends to keep his feelings private and grows uncomfortable when people probe his private life. He prefers to tackle the task at hand rather than focus on personal relations. Not known for tact, he builds a wall around his soul life which can make him insensitive to the feelings of others. He may make sarcastic or sharp comments without realizing the hurt these cause. Yet within his own soul walls, he is supersensitive and easily hurt when others say something unkind to him. He then withdraws and takes refuge in his inner sanctum of safety, projecting coldness and unapproachability. Thus the Spiritual Investigator may lock himself in an ivory tower and approach life in a narrow-minded way.

Spiritual Investigators often have a difficult time. They long to be acknowledged and to feel other people's interest in them. Often their talents remain undeveloped because they require so much patience from others. Yet they feel unrecognized and resent those whose quickness or social ease brings them recognition. When they have ventured out and enjoyed success, they have trouble letting go of the experience and want to repeat it again and again.

With support, encouragement and lots of time, the Spiritual Investigator can let go of the past and move into the present. He can step out of his inner world and converse with the outer. In Greek mythology, the god Kronos – called Saturn by the Romans – saw his own children as rivals and swallowed them, because he was afraid of losing his power and position to them. We can see a parallel to this with some Spiritual Investigators who show intense jealousy of those who are appreciated and honored while they are not.

The Spiritual Investigator has an important role in a group. Because he wants to find the truth, he will contemplate an issue until he achieves insight. At the same time, his strong connection to memory can work against him. For example, if a co-worker makes a mistake, he will probably not forget it. Everything is filed away. Despite his stubbornness, his conclusions may turn out to be right. However, his sense of righteousness can create an unpleasant mood. Given responsibility to lead a group, he may possibly get stuck looking for the deeper meaning behind every decision or weighing all the variables. Then the group has difficulty getting anything done.

Spiritual Investigators work best when they can have some space around them, and from time to time can contribute profound observations from their research. They often have wonderful ideas but lack the ability to get their ideas considered. Often they are passed over while someone else's ideas are taken more seriously, even though the Spiritual Investigator's insights are needed by the group. One such man did his doctoral thesis on something which no one else was interested in at the time. Only ten years later this subject was recognized as important By then, though, he had been passed over.

It is important for Spiritual Investigators to learn to relax. They find this difficult because they are often awkward and uncomfortable in their bodies. For instance, they are typically not very comfortable being touched, so that massage or physical affection are not easily accepted. It is important for them to get out of themselves and experience lightness. This is most possible in nature. Hiking and gardening can be therapeutic for them.

Because they have difficulty letting go or relaxing, they don't easily go out of control. But they do get stuck in fixed ideas and have trouble letting go of them. Since they often replay these ideas over and over in their minds, they can be vulnerable to depression.

The Spiritual Investigator needs warmth. Either he will respond positively to it by expanding and being brought out of his deepest recesses into social interaction or he will feel threatened and withdraw from it. Usually, he is unable to produce much warmth on his own, but he longs for it. A strong melancholic mood often accompanies this soul quality, fixing the person in his inner world. Even when he withdraws from warmth which is offered, he still wants it, but he may become stubborn and reject it. We have to continually offer warmth to Spiritual Investigators, even though we may be rejected. Sooner or later, they will respond (even if they claim that they do so only to please us). If we don't offer them warmth, they will remember that also and hold it as a grudge (see appendix).

Spiritual Investigators bear a heavy weight on their shoulders; some take their serious burdens in their stride and go forward, while others are crushed by them. We can see this when we look at elderly people. Some have been made stronger by what they have had to bear, while others, unable to bear the weight of their destinies, lose their joy in living and become recluses.

The immature Spiritual Investigator can be self-centered and stubborn as he clings to the past or focuses only on himself. He can become cantankerous, egotistical, suspicious, remote, and bitter. Although he may be a source of important information, he may also be so single-mindedly involved in his research or thoughts that he misses its relevance to the community.

Spiritual Investigators as adolescents

Adolescents with this soul type have a difficult time. They have some characteristics of old age and not many of youth. In fact, they often have difficulty making friends and may feel isolated. It is difficult to reach Spiritual Investigator adolescents because they are introverts who only occasionally come from behind their screens. When they do, however, they have a great deal to say, but not always in the kindest way. Pure Spiritual Investigators are not common in teenager circles, so they usually stand out in their one-sidedness.

They deeply and thoughtfully take in what is taught. However, they are not usually willing to give it back in class discussion or in written form. Although they don't communicate often, they usually have profound comments to make, yet their profundity doesn't always reach beyond the level of talk. They tend to be slow and ponderous, attributes which don't lend themselves to social interaction. They are put off by having to react quickly and will not complete work if they feel caught off guard. They need to develop flexibility, but this is very difficult for this soul type.

Spiritual Investigators are at home when they are doing research – concentrating on material, penetrating a subject in depth. Their ability to concentrate while doggedly pursuing a topic allows them to be effective.

Anecdote: Robert

Robert had done extensive research into cave paintings. He mentioned this to his high school art history teacher and offered to share his knowledge with the class. Since Robert didn't often volunteer, the teacher enthusiastically agreed that he could have fifteen minutes of the next day's lesson. After fifteen minutes, however, Robert did not stop. In fact, he was annoyed when the bell interrupted his presentation, even though he had been speaking for an hour. He never noticed that he had lost his classmates' attention long before. His teacher had felt reluctant to stop him for fear of discouraging his future participation. Robert's comment after class was that he had more information than he'd been able to give.

Spiritual Investigator adolescents such as Robert experience excitement in the realm of thinking. At the same time, they lack the spontaneity, daring, and foolhardiness which we often associate with youth.

Mature Spiritual Investigators

Through the active working of their 'I', Spiritual Investigators are able to penetrate their one-sided inwardness and transform it. For example, a Spiritual Investigator may be a specialist in a particular species of tree, becoming deeply focused on this to the exclusion of everything else. At a certain point he realizes that to truly understand the tree he needs to also consider the climate, the ecosystem, the impact on the tree of changes in the broader environment. To address the full complexity of the phenomena, he must collaborate with other researchers. When the Spiritual Investigator moves his thinking from a one-sided focus on his speciality to a broader perspective, he is transforming his soul type and becoming more balanced. The transformed Spiritual Investigator uses his ability to think and to do research for the benefit of the earth and humanity.

Through his spiritual efforts, the mature Spiritual Investigator becomes a listener who offers comments when they are wanted rather than overpowering others with his thoughts. He is able to gain perspective, laugh at himself at times. Through his spiritual efforts, he can develop wisdom which becomes a blessing to those around him. This attracts people to him.

When a Spiritual Investigator is given time and recognition, he becomes better able to place his gifts of thoroughness and profound reflection at the service of the group. In addition to time, he needs freedom and acceptance to work things out in the way he does best. What is needed is not indifference but understanding of the difficult position the Spiritual Investigator finds himself in.

Whereas the one-sided Spiritual Investigator thinks in rather a fixed, rote fashion, repeating what has gone before, the balanced Spiritual Investigator is awake to a new kind of thinking in which the spiritual element renews, enlivens, sheds light on, and helps him focus on the human condition.

Then the Spiritual Investigator, with eyes cast down and focused on the dusty, printed page, is able to look up to the heavens and become an investigator of the spirit. His sense of responsibility brings great strength as he takes his spiritual work very seriously.

Another aspect of the transformed Spiritual Investigator is that he feels pain. He is up against obstacles which only he may be able to see. We must acknowledge this sincerely. When he can transform his sensitivity to his own pain into a sensitivity to the suffering of others, deep resources of compassion begin flowing in him. His sensitivity is then turned outward, instead of only on himself.

In the 60s and beyond

When people reach their sixties and beyond, they often exhibit the qualities associated with Spiritual Investigators. They mull over the past, sometimes getting lost in what has been and might have been. They remember people who played a special part in their lives, who did a kind deed, who acknowledged them. They may research their family tree or reconnect with relatives they haven't seen in decades. They enjoy reminiscing with friends about their early years.

What is happening in these later years? People are trying to come to terms with their destinies, and the Spiritual Investigator qualities – introversion, depth of thinking, and living in memories – serve them well, regardless of what their own dominant soul type may be.

As Spiritual Investigators grow older, the rest of their generation, in effect, 'catches up' with where the Spiritual Investigator has been all along, and the Spiritual Investigator no longer seems so different.

Chapter 5. The Reflective Preserver

Reflective Preservers tend to be thorough, systematic, dependable people, sensible and realistic. We can feel assured that they won't go off on some wild goose chase. Reflective Preservers are concerned that activities are recorded and documented so the facts will be known. They help us focus on the actual events or facts before letting our feelings affect our perceptions.

Reflective Preservers have very good memories and are good at quoting facts or what a particular authority has said. They often have ready knowledge of statistics. Their excellent memory for details can be very impressive, although when asked to relate these statistics to a broad topic, they falter. They are often less interested in the meaning behind the facts or statistics than in the satisfaction of quoting the facts themselves.

They know the 'right way' to do things, and find it difficult to change routine. If coffee break is at 10:15 every morning, it should not be changed. That is the way it is. If they've done something a particular way for ten years, they should continue doing it this way. Precedent is very important in determining the future. Trying something new or being spontaneous makes Reflective Preservers uncomfortable. Over time, they can consider something new, but at first they distrust it.

The one-sided Reflective Preserver may know a lot about outer things but be rather empty inside. A tendency to stay on the surface of things creates a superficial quality that puts great emphasis on appearances.

When we want someone to be accurate down to the last detail, we should seek out a Reflective Preserver. We can trust her efforts in such tasks as bookkeeping or being secretary of a group. We know that she is organized. She works steadily and stays on schedule. Even if it means working all night, she will make the numbers balance. She is a stickler for perfection.

She is more comfortable in the world of concepts than with her emotions. In fact, she is often suspicious of people who express their feelings too openly. This is partly because the Reflective Preserver respects only those who are similar to herself and also because she is insecure with people who are unpredictable.

In a position of responsibility, she wants employees who follow rules, who do their jobs in predictable, responsible ways. She wants to know what is actually going to happen, not what may happen or what new ideas are lurking in the background. She seldom encourages innovation and sees little value in creative brainstorming sessions. This causes problems because she tends to focus on short-term tasks without much interest in the long term. When confronted with ideas for change, she is slow to grasp their importance. Because she expects the job to get done as a matter of course, she seldom praises those working with or for her. Thus a gap can develop between the Reflective Preserver and her colleagues or employees.

She is impressed by intelligence since she is very proud of her own abilities as well. The danger for the Reflective Preserver is that her intellect can be cold and untouched by compassion. If she is going to truly transform her thinking, she needs to penetrate beyond concepts to a living reality.

Other Reflective Preservers express their emphasis on appearance by over-valuing good looks, clothes and cars. This is different from those Reflective Preservers who are quite happy to get a car just like the one they had before, or who dress the same way they have been dressing for twenty years. One-sided Reflective Preservers who are more attracted to glitz and glamor take a superficial approach to life and often have difficulty entering into relationships of any depth. Because of their emphasis on romance for its own sake, we might call them Romantic Preservers. They tend to sentimentality rather than balanced feelings.

Reflective Preservers as adolescents

The main quality of adolescents who are Reflective Preservers is imitation. Unconsciously they mimic the gestures, expressions, and actions of others. Taking on the latest fad, mirroring the way certain people in the school dress, using particular phrases, are all ways in which teenagers express the Reflective Preserver soul quality.

They are often very attentive students, taking in what is taught, receiving what the teacher has to give. They don't necessarily get their written work done, but they are very good at listening and giving back what the teacher has said, often word for word. They also unconsciously drink in much that is told to them, which may come to light only years later. Their book knowledge and oral retention are impressive. They remember details, even trivia. They often do well on short answer and multiple choice tests because they hold the information so well, but they don't do as well on essays, because they have difficulty penetrating material and coming to conclusions.

The Reflective Preserver typically responds strongly to the atmosphere around her and imitates it. If it is harmonious, she is peaceful. If it is chaotic, she becomes nervous. This appears to those around her as rigidity because she seems unable to hold her own center in the midst of change.

It is difficult for them to be flexible enough to sustain and nurture personal relationships. Unwilling to bend, to make exceptions, or to see individual needs, Reflective Preservers stick to the rules, no matter what. They are sticklers for precision and argue in lawyerly fashion about any deviations from the rules. Changes in schedule or in assignments cause them discomfort and they react petulantly or aggressively.

They can be unaware of what is going on around them, if friends are having difficulty, if there are problems, or if someone is trying to manipulate them. They tend to take things literally, missing the subtlety of a situation.

The passivity of the Reflective Preserver can cause her to become self-indulgent. She takes in what comes to her. If she is hungry and there is much rich food around, she will often eat without limit. The same is true in connection with other self-indulgences. She likes life to be pleasant and soft.

How can we work with the Reflective Preserver adolescent? She has a quiet, contemplative approach to life, and takes time to think things through before making decisions.

The teacher or other adult can help her by insisting that her work goes beyond the superficial. The more the adult can penetrate to the real person, the more helpful this is. The adult has to really love the young person and go past the outer reflections to the individuality beneath. Often the Reflective Preserver is the 'good' teenager who does everything right, learns well, is a model student – and is ignored. Yet there are problems in her soul life which need attending to. It is helpful to draw Reflective Preservers into the outer world. They need to observe, to understand the world, and come to love it.

It is tempting to accelerate the Reflective Preserver in school. To the outer eye, she seems to learn quickly, but over time we find that her learning is rather 'parrot-fashion'. She may retain details but is less successful in developing the big picture and achieving a deep level of understanding. Some of these teenagers are labeled 'brains', even before their teen years. They would rather memorize facts than go out and do physical exercise. By the time these children enter adolescence, this tendency may be quite pronounced. We often spot them because they avoid relationships. They are more at home with their computers, with building models and playing video games than they are at doing things with friends. Only when they feel very safe will they relax and share themselves with others. Parents should resist showing off their precocious Reflective Preserver children, and instead encourage them to try new experiences and new ways of doing things.

The Reflective Preserver preserves images for a long time and reflects them in later years. If she has had a problematic childhood, anger or bitterness may remain for a long time, as she will remember the details vividly. On the other hand, if a Reflective Preserver has a beautiful childhood filled with reverence and awe, that is what she will reflect in later years. Whatever gestures or kindness were shown to her will be remembered and will become an important foundation as she begins to transform this soul attitude.

Mature Reflective Preservers

As the Reflective Preserver works to transform her soul quality, she learns there are times to bend and become flexible.

Although it is not easy at first, she is able to call upon her memory without being at the mercy of it. When she speaks about the history of a group or of an initiative, she will find others seeking her out to learn about the past. She is admired for her memory of who was there at the beginning, how things started, and what colorful anecdotes exist about the people.

They will enjoy her stories and compliment her on her ability to remember details.

Mature Reflective Preservers are good at evaluating a process because they are so good at reflecting what has happened. Their clarity is a gift to the group. When a group is too caught up in emotions and judgments, it is often the Reflective Preserver who brings the group back to focus by insisting on getting the facts correct first. As long as she is not too rigid, she helps keep the group focused, and her objectivity is welcomed.

Her thoroughness serves the needs of the group but no longer is compulsive. While she is valued for her dependability, she performs in a balanced way, allowing herself time to relax and enjoy herself rather than developing an ulcer in her attempt to be perfect.

The mature Reflective Preserver pays more attention to depth than to the surface. She can differentiate between gently reminding her friends or partner that something has to be done, and becoming a compulsive nagger.

Two qualities that help the Reflective Preserver broaden her perspective are humor and interest. The more she can lighten up by not taking herself so seriously, the more effectively she can function socially. When she can laugh and say, 'There I go again', she is on the way to transforming her one-sidedness. She can cultivate genuine interest in other people as a way of deepening her connections with people.

Chapter 6.
The Thinker Organizer

Thinker Organizers bring clarity and wisdom into life. Like Jupiter or Zeus, mythical ruler of the heavens and earth, the Thinker Organizer sees the entire picture and orders the details into a whole. He has a strong inner life from which flows wisdom, but he also has a strong command of what happens in the present. Full of enthusiasm for the way things need to be brought together, the Thinker Organizer contributes to the well-being of a group.

Many like to rely on Thinker Organizers because they make life orderly and sensible. Things get done on time. There are reasons for everything they do. Thinker Organizers love systems and gadgets that help bring order. They like to bring flip charts to meetings, to bring movement into static diagrams, to systematize what resists being put into boxes. They like timetables and schedules, symmetry and structure.

Confident that everything will work out, Thinker Organizers instill hope in those around them. Yet they can go too far and become haughty or carry out the rules rigidly, leaving little room for exceptional circumstances. They want outer life to conform to inner laws. If they are too one-sided, their certainty about how things should be done may develop into arrogance. They order the world to their liking. In such a case, the 'subjects' may feel exploited or manipulated and develop resentment against their 'high and mighty' ruler. From his vantage point, the Thinker Organizer presents the big picture for a project, a book, a theater production. Although he may be very competent at defining strategy, he also may need someone to follow up on the details.

Because Thinker Organizers have a tendency to be philosophical, they can get lost in the beauty of an idea and not bring it down to reality. Warmth and graciousness can take a back seat to concentration and thought. Loyalty to the truth, however defined, motivates the Thinker Organizer.

In Greek mythology, Zeus was the child of Kronos and ruler of Olympus. Challenged by the Titans and Giants, Zeus battled the new gods, casting thunderbolts until the air was filled with fury and the earth shuddered and burned. Only when wisdom had overcome disorder was Zeus able to reign in harmony. Usually, the Thinker Organizer seems cool and composed, but beneath the surface there lies a rage that can boil up and erupt if his domain is challenged directly or if good and right are in jeopardy. A group may experience this fury when the Thinker Organizer's 'great wisdom' is challenged or disbelieved.

'How dare they question my wisdom? Don't they understand that I know what will happen if we pursue the present course?' From on high, with arrogance, he bestows pronouncements on the group. All is well as long as these edicts are respected and obeyed, but when they are not, the Thinker Organizer is in disbelief and needs to convince the group of his wisdom.

The more he is ignored or challenged, the more frustrated he grows, until finally in a torrent of invective and condescending insults, he storms out. This comes as a shock, because the Thinker Organizer is usually cool and controlled, living in the rarified air of thought.

It is easy to confuse the Thinker Organizer with the Spiritual Investigator. A big difference is that the Thinker Organizer wants to get things done while the Spiritual Investigator is content to immerse himself in the past or to dig deeply for the essence without moving into action. We can also confuse Thinker Organizers with Active Talkers because both want to make things happen in the world. The Thinker Organizer tries to balance thinking and doing, while the Active Talker usually connects deeds with power rather than with ideas.

Thinker Organizer as adolescent

In adolescence, Thinker Organizers need challenges such as difficult problems to solve, leadership opportunities, and organizational responsibilities. When these strong individuals don't have challenges, they grow bored and become critical and arrogant.

These young people take hold of a subject, an oral report, or a research project, and throw themselves into it, heart and soul. They may do much more than is required, either because they have become so interested in the subject or to impress the teacher. However, they expect to be recognized for their efforts.

The strength of these overachieving teenagers is also their weakness. Confident that they can handle many activities at once, they take on too much, often pushing themselves until they get sick. The reality is that they are good at making things happen and they do feel responsible. Helping them sort out the essential from the non-essential aids them in achieving balance in their lives.

These are the teenagers who organize high school events, who design a constitution for student government, who draft policy statements for the teachers to consider. They are leaders who have many good ideas even if they don't have the strength to convince others or to carry through. But they love bringing order into chaos. Generally optimistic, they express confidence and hope in the future. Their friends admire them for their deep inner strength. On the negative side, the teenaged Thinker Organizer can be arrogant and unreasonable if challenged.

Mature Thinker Organizers

The one-sided Thinker Organizer has difficulty with compromise. He will hold his own position, even to the point of insisting on having his way, simply because he's sure that he is right. The mature Thinker Organizer, however, can integrate subjective and objective aspects of his personality and achieve wisdom and foresight. We need mature Thinker Organizers for their ability to see the whole picture, the grand design. We admire their intelligence and their organizational skills.

As Thinker Organizers mellow, their horizons expand, yielding a broader view of life. Many of their earlier prejudices fall by the wayside as they grow more tolerant and good-hearted, which allows them to be more forgiving, more generous to those around them. They develop greater respect for others, and we can become more sympathetic to them at this time. As a result, judgment becomes clearer and more objective.

Thinker Organizers need to cultivate qualities of compassion and humility, enabling them to become more approachable and accessible. When they develop a sense of humility, they find that their peers appreciate them and trust them.

Between forty–nine to fifty–six, people generally bring a broader perspective to life, seeing the whole picture. In other words, they come to resemble the Thinker Organizer. During this period, it is natural to yearn for wisdom rather than for mere knowledge. If the 'I' actively penetrates the soul, one's thinking gradually becomes more mobile and vigorous, clearer and more light-filled.

Thinker Organizers at any age, and many adults of other soul types during the 49-to-56 years, think before they act. Instead of pressuring others to do things their way, they are able to calmly state their position. If they fail to convince, they accept their differences. In William Wordsworth's words, these are the 'years that bring the philosophic mind'. Reverence and devotion open the soul to new possibilities. It becomes a priority for most maturing adults to give attention to their spiritual development.

Mature Thinker Organizers enhance their relationships, bringing broad perspective and grasping the essential elements.

Chapter 7.
The Social Innovator

The Social Innovator is a very flexible person. She keeps things going with humor and with a hundred and one ideas, some of which are brilliant while others are ridiculous. A lover of new possibilities, the Social Innovator can't stand things being done in the same way, year after year. Unlike the Thinker Organizer who makes order out of chaos, the Social Innovator enjoys stirring up a bit of chaos. Her strength and enthusiasm lie in communication and connecting people with one another.

Like mercury or quicksilver, the Social Innovator adapts to different situations, saying one thing to this person, talking to that person, trying to make things work out.

In Roman mythology Mercury is the winged messenger of the gods. Sometimes he brings messages that resolve or heal a situation, other times he creates mischief through deception. The ability to adapt easily, to keep life in movement is a special quality of the Social Innovators.

When they are well balanced and operating at their highest level, Social Innovators bring healing powers to those with whom they come in contact. They bring what is static into movement. New ideas are tried, life is interesting. People are brought together who need to meet each other. Social Innovators are excellent coordinators. Through them, the social realm is brought into balance. These mercurial people love to make things happen and then stand selflessly back and enjoy other people getting along and inspiring each other. Working behind the scenes, they are interested in the world, but they are not going to force themselves on it. They listen just long enough to get the point and understand what is needed. They buzz around, dropping a joke here, a pun there, keeping the interaction light and flexible. They are easy to get along with and easily forgiven.

In a group dynamic in which the members can't find a new way to look at a problem, the Social Innovator offers a special gift. She suggests many different approaches to help them attain their goals. This inner flexibility can be just what is needed. In this sense, Social Innovators are realists. They sense what will work and offer it. However, they can go too far with their spontaneity. Led by feelings and circumstances of the moment, a Social Innovator may prove unpredictable and come up with wild schemes. Her strength is her cleverness, while her weakness is that she may be dishonest as she tells different things to different people.

These Social Innovator qualities serve well in professions that require the ability to move from one person to another and get along easily with many different kinds of people, such as in sales jobs, public relations, and communications.

The Social Innovator who is too one-sided, may become superficial, flitting about, thriving on gossip, and having trouble committing to any one position. She needs to slow down and become more conscious of her actions. When she begins to pay more attention to her behavior, she can become thoughtful and conscious.

The Social Innovator typically needs to develop a stronger center as well as greater direction and inner certainty. She needs to work on developing concentration. A helpful exercise is to observe something, then reflect on it. For example, she can choose an ordinary object such as a pencil and try to concentrate on it for one minute, then two, and eventually up to five minutes. What is a pencil? What material is it made of? What shape is it? How is it used? Etc. As simple as this may seem, it is difficult for most people to maintain focus, and it's particularly challenging for the Social Innovator. All kinds of extraneous thoughts enter. Phrases from songs or conversations, memories of things that need to be done, images of people's faces or of favorite activities intervene in the act of concentration. It takes will to exclude them and to continue focusing on the pencil. Such will exercise helps build a strong and focused center.

Another helpful exercise for the Social Innovator is to reflect daily on her actions. Going back over what she did during the day, imagining herself as she progressed from one activity to another, slows down her frenetic activity and brings conscious thought into what otherwise is a scattered and disconnected series of unconscious actions. This exercise is helpful for bringing inner discipline. Progress may seem slow at first, but after a while she will realize that she is more in control of herself.

Light-hearted flitting about is natural for people of all soul types during the years from seven to fourteen. The natural enthusiasm and butterfly quality of childhood are the same qualities as the Social Innovator at its strongest. Those who can keep this quality alive and bring it into balance as they mature bring charm and delight as well as intuitive insight to those around them.

Because the Social Innovator gets pulled in all directions by what is going on, she needs friends who will help her focus so she can realize her highest possibilities.

The Social Innovator as adolescent

It is not difficult to recognize the Social Innovators in a high school classroom. They are the social butterflies, enthusiastic and bubbly. They may be cheerleaders or the students who have lots of ideas in student council meetings, or those who bounce from one thing to another. They are refreshing and delightful. They are also the ones who think that they can do anything and, consequently, take on too much. Unlike Thinker Organizers, the Social Innovator does not have so strong an organizing capacity nor the will to follow through. Consequently, when she is overwhelmed by too many requirements and distractions, she often has difficulty staying with her tasks and finishing them. She may start a homework assignment several times, but misplace it. Scattered in her thinking, frustrated in her will, she tries to get by on charm, but that works only briefly. Very persuasively, she comes up with all kinds of excuses, some convincing. Social Innovators are difficult to resist at first. They have the skills of the supersalesperson who can talk you into anything.

The Social Innovator often has a kind of sixth sense for what kinds of things will work. Her intuition is keen. The Social Innovator tends to be a popular teen, charismatic, with a ready smile and a knowing ability to make her way around. When she arrives at a dance or walks into the cafeteria, there is action. She sparks excitement and liveliness. It is fun to be around her, and other teenagers flock to her. However, she can also spark envy in those who do not get the same response.

The Social Innovator can also be the instigator of mischief. She teems with so many ideas that some are bound to be troublemaking. When we observe a certain sparkle in her eyes, we suspect that she is up to something, and we may well be right! When confronted about it, she may charm her way out of accepting responsibility.

Frustrated teachers try to pin down those Social Innovators who rely too much on charm to get through high school. Their ability to make friends can both help and hinder them. If their friends are like them, they have the added strength of numbers to try to avoid meeting their responsibilities. If some of their loyal friends are other soul types, however, those friends may help the Social Innovator to wake up and take responsibility. They can hold her to her commitments, do homework with her, make sure that she gets her assignments in, and offer the support that helps the Social Innovator transform previous habits.

Teachers can help by giving her responsibility for a project or an event and then offering support to follow through. If the responsibility is given without the support, the student will most likely fail; but if the teacher stands by the student, not doing the work for her but thinking it through with her, setting frequent deadlines for small parts of the task, showing the student how to be successful, then new possibilities can arise. One of the greatest learning tools for the Social Innovator is painful experience. But we need not try to inflict pain on our young Social Innovators, as life itself will take care of this.

The adolescent Social Innovator carries her childhood qualities too strongly into adolescence. Many of the qualities which I have described are appropriate in children, especially from seven to fourteen, but we expect some maturity to develop as they reach adolescence. When teenagers continue acting immaturely instead of moving into the next phase, we see the Social Innovator's negative side.

Mature Social Innovators

While we can see the difficulties described above carried over into adult life, we can also see the great gifts which the Social Innovator brings to a community. The special quality of this soul type is one which we all need in some degree. To be social human beings, we need to know how to reach out to others, to be lively, to know how to communicate.

The mature Social Innovator has made many friends and has had a variety of experiences. She has learned to deepen her relationships rather than flit from one to another. She is able to stay with an experience long enough to benefit from it. She finishes what she starts, and she is dependable. Yet she never loses her charm.

She is able to employ her 'people skills' for altruistic purposes. She enjoys getting people together. Her ability to sense what people need allows her to help them. She makes people feel at ease, even in difficult circumstances.

She still enjoys change but now it is because change is needed, rather than just to stir things up.

The balanced Social Innovator lights up our lives, brings movement into what is stuck, and healing to those who need it.

Chapter 8.
The Radiant Balancer

The Radiant Balancer is like the golden sun, bestowing warmth and light. Radiant Balancers are bringers of harmony. Able to reconcile opposite points of view, they come up with creative ideas and solutions. They assess situations and bring insight to them. This type is characterized by light of understanding and warmth of heart.

Radiant Balancers bring together the positive aspects of the other six soul types. Their feelings and intellect work beautifully together. Their actions are righteous, their hearts full of goodness. Does the Radiant Balancer have a negative side? Yes: when everything is in such a state of balance, lethargy and inertia can set in.

In the world of metals, it is gold which has the qualities of warmth and light. Unlike other metals, which are altered by rust and weathering, gold maintains its luster and its malleability. It is an excellent conductor of heat and electricity. Thus gold can be a metaphor for balance and beauty, and for the soul qualities of the Radiant Balancer.

The Radiant Balancer as a soul type can be seen on two levels: as a distinct soul attitude in itself and also as a culmination that each of the other soul types is moving toward. The Radiant Balancer quality lies seedlike within each gesture, but it is expressed only when there has been transformation. In the fairy tale *Rumpelstiltskin*, the miller's daughter had to spin straw into gold. Metaphorically, we might say that she had to transform her lower qualities or her one-sidedness, into the highest qualities of the Radiant Balancer. To do so she first needed to develop qualities which were quite alien to her, which were embodied in the spiky and scheming intellect of Rumpelstiltskin.

We also can look at the seventh quality as a sun quality, which we all have and which shines on each of the other qualities, bringing out its finest aspects. In a group, we need the best attributes of each of these six other soul types.

Let's look at what each contributes.

The Active Talker makes sure that the group decides what has to be done, then leads the group into battle, much as warriors go off defending their cause. He doesn't mince words but makes his intentions clear. Active Talkers are the ones who get pushed forward to speak for the group. Without them, the group would spin its wheels searching for an appropriate solution.

The Dreamy Nurturer cares about the other members of the group. He senses when one of the group is in pain and is there to support him. It is more important for the Dreamy Nurturer that the group feels good about itself than that it reaches its goal. He wants the members of the group to share their feelings, to find ways of talking to each other in a supportive way so that no one gets hurt feelings. He creates a warm and loving environment in which a room looks cosy, giving attention to those little details that bring beauty into everyone's life.

The Thinker Organizer is needed to rescue the group from drowning in detail. He strives for the big picture, he plans and organizes, he figures out who does what and when. His skills are needed for every project the group involves itself in. The Thinker Organizer needs time to work this out. He has to be left alone for a while for everything to become clear. Then he is ready to share his plan with others. Thinker Organizers shine their wisdom on the group so that something new may develop that reveals the group's highest intention.

The Social Innovator saves the day with humor and with the ability to get the various members talking to each other. He loosens up others when they become stuck in their positions. His ability to live in the moment leaves him free to move flexibly. His inner adaptability and the way he produces just enough chaos to make life interesting makes him a necessary member of the group.

The Spiritual Investigator brings everyone back to the starting point. He wants to know the purpose of every action and needs to be sure that it is essential. He can drive other members to distraction because he is not ready to move until he has the facts, all the facts. When he figures out what it's all about, however, the group benefits from his clear focus and ability to distinguish the essential from the non-essential.

The Reflective Preserver keeps the records, the archives, and can produce them at a moment's notice. He reminds the group to stay with its safe, traditional approach based on what was done the year before. When others become too flighty, the Reflective Preserver holds things steady.

When all these attributes are present in a group, the group manifests the gesture of **Radiant Balancer.** The attributes of the Radiant Balancer are also most apparent in everyone's life between ages 21 and 42, a period of three seven-year cycles. Each of those seven-year phases is dominated by one of the above soul-types, but the 'sun' shines on all three cycles:

Between twenty-one and forty-two, we can harmonize the soul forces of feeling, thinking, and willing.

Between twenty-one and twenty-eight, our feelings are very strong and influence decisions and attitudes. By the end of this period, however, feelings should have been balanced and transformed.

Between twenty-eight and thirty-five, thinking is the dominant soul force. By the end of this period decisions should be arrived at through careful thought rather than by impulsive feelings.

Between thirty-five and forty-two, we are challenged to understand our actions, becoming more conscious of what choices we make, being more objective in directing our will. Through this activity the will becomes transformed.

If we can use these years between twenty-one and forty-two to balance the inner and outer expressions of thinking, feeling, and willing, then we can benefit from a deepening spiritual awareness after age forty-two. Our sense of self will be heightened, not in egotism, but in caring interaction with the rest of society.

The Radiant Balancer as adolescent

We have probably all met teenagers who are so beautifully balanced that we cannot find any fault in them. They are even known as 'golden girls' and 'golden boys'. They are excellent students, polite, responsible, mature, and at ease socially. We come to expect this behavior from them at all times. If they falter and behave in a less than perfect way, we are disappointed and wonder what the problem is. Such high expectations can become a trap for these Radiant Balancer teenagers.

They may wake up one day when they are sixteen or seventeen and realize they have not been having much fun, that they have not rebelled against the adult world, that they have not disobeyed or been mischievous or in any way 'rocked the boat'.

They may resent that their teachers and parents have treated them as adults (even though they enjoyed being treated like this) and thus have put an undue burden on them. These are often the young people in whom adults confide or whom they pump for information about other teenagers. One such young man had long been the 'golden boy' of his class. When he was sixteen, he spent a summer in Europe and had a relationship with an older woman. Returning home, he was in full rebellion. He carried on in an outrageous way, did poor schoolwork, stayed out late at night, and was restless. He confused all those who had come to expect exemplary behavior from him. It took him several years to regain balance, but when he did it was a balance which he had worked for and achieved himself.

One girl consciously decided not to hand in a major assignment to the teacher to test whether the teacher would treat her objectively and give her a failing grade for the course. She had always been conscientious, but now she wanted to have the feeling of being 'bad'.

Radiant Balancer adolescents often skip the familiar teenage rebellion of ninth and tenth grades, coming, instead to their rebellious period after sixteen when they have greater power because their intellects have ripened. Now, when they attack the adult world, they do it with sharpness of thinking, knowing just how to deflate or wound. Their anger and disappointment are more powerful than if they were younger and more awkward. Just as their classmates are growing out of rebelliousness and settling down to a more balanced sense of priorities, this group gets going. This often throws them off balance for longer because it affects them just as they are preparing for college or their first serious job. On the other hand, they have more perspective and a clearer sense of identity than they did at fourteen or fifteen.

As adults, we can help Radiant Balancer adolescents by being aware of our expectations and our way of approaching them. We should not overly praise them in front of others but accept them for who they are. Holding them up as models for the other students can be a burden for them in the long run.

Radiant Balancer adolescents are always a little ahead of themselves, being adult before they reach the adult years. The natural time to come into this period is between twenty-one and forty-two, when we strive to be balanced out of the activity of our own 'I'. Then we can strive for the purity of gold in our actions and hope to shine and radiate love to all those around us.

Chapter 9. Integrating the Seven Soul Qualities

The seven soul qualities weave together to create a mood within an individual or within a group. Depending on whether the strengths or weaknesses of the soul quality predominates, the mood changes. First let us recall the strength of each of the soul qualities and see how this contributes to effective group dynamics and the accomplishment of goals.

Spiritual Investigators find deep meaning, go to the heart of a matter, can see into the distant past and forward into the future, and bring a spiritual dimension into the physical. They bring a willingness to persevere until the truth is identified. They bring equanimity.

Thinker Organizers conceive plans and realize them, organizing from a broad view, taking many aspects into account. Spiritually objective, they bring clarity, perspective, and wisdom to a group .

Dreamy Nurturers listen well, care for people, bring modesty and beauty, and nurture the group's feeling life. They bring to the group compassion, empathy, and sympathy.

Social Innovators are flexible, creative, and shake loose the established way of operating so that new things can happen. They bring people together through networking. They bring spontaneity and they interest the group in new things. Through their intuitive understanding, they often facilitate healing between people.

Reflective Preservers have objective memories, strong intellect, and are knowledgable. They are good at reflecting back what has happened and carry traditions in the social life. They bring accuracy and precision to the group.

Active Talkers are creative, directed, and bold. They bring order, keep momentum, and discipline their will. They exemplify courage and strength. Willing to take risks and assert themselves, they make excellent leaders.

Radiant Balancers bring insight and warmth, are harmonious, and bring the best out of others. They often integrate the viewpoints of all the members of the group.

Becoming effective means bringing together the best of each of these qualities.

In the same order as above, we have the following abilities:
1. Grasping the deeper meaning.
2. Planning.
3. Caring for people's feelings.
4. Keeping things flexible, bringing people together.
5. Documenting what we are doing.
6. Action! Doing.
7. Keeping everything in balance.

Now let us look at what happens when the weaknesses of these soul qualities dominate instead of the strengths.

Spiritual Investigators are too inward and narrow-minded. They hide themselves in an ivory tower, get lost in problem-solving. They are anti-social and find it difficult to compromise.

Thinker Organizers are too abstract, theoretical, rigid, and lacking in humor. They get caught up in structure and lose sight of the meaning and purpose of the overall plan.

Dreamy Nurturers are overly concerned with process and forget the need to have a result; they get lost in illusions, and lose track of time. They can be too focused on aesthetics at the expense of practical realities such as cost, time, energy, and the feasibility of their plans.

Social Innovators are too wishy-washy and cannot stand up for a principle. They are too adaptable and won't commit to a structure. They try to use humor to relieve tension, but may miss the mark and just upset everyone.

Reflective Preservers reflect what other people are saying, but don't think for themselves. They remain superficial. They get stuck on tradition and precedent. They become fussy about details.

Active Talkers are impatient, want action above all, see the goal as more important than the process, are aggressive and bossy, and impose themselves on others.

Radiant Balancers become lethargic and don't see the need to change what is working well.

Things go wrong when the worst aspect of each quality comes out.
1. Narrow minded.
2. Too theoretical.
3. Stuck on process.
4. Unable to make commitments.
5. Stuck on tradition.
6. Too aggressive.
7. Lethargic

When we understand the value of our soul quality strengths, we have a target to aim for. Then we can engage in an effort to transform our weaknesses for the benefit of the group, and for our own development.

Chapter 10: The Seven Soul Qualities as a Path of Understanding

So far in this section, we have explored the soul types as aspects of individual personality, as qualities which we all have and can draw on, and as influences which are particularly strong during certain stages of life. However, there is an additional way to look at the soul types – as a path of understanding. The seven soul types are all capacities which we can develop in order either to understand another human being or to develop spiritual insight. If we wish to do this, we must activate the forces of our 'I'.

Using the seven soul gestures as a way of understanding another person

By using this path of understanding, we can become better observers of children, partners, friends and family members, and overcome personality conflicts.

Reflective Preserver approach

Observe the physical features of another person during the day. Were his eyes blue or brown? Was he long waisted? Big boned? Delicately featured?

In the evening, try to remember his physical features. The next day, observe again and correct what was vague the night before.

Keep working on this perception and memory exercise until it is accurate. It is important to be objective and keep feelings from coloring the memory of the physical features.

Dreamy Nurturer approach

Experience the beauty of the other. Notice what is particularly harmonious and pleasing about him. By doing this repeatedly, a sense of reverence is developed. This is particularly important in overcoming antipathy or hostility to another person.

Social Innovator approach

Think of him, using simile, metaphor or analogy. For example, 'This person is like an oak with strong roots deeply anchored in the ground', or 'This person is like a birch that sways in the wind.' You also can use comparisons with animals, colors, or geographical features to gain a greater sense of what he is like. For example,

'He is like a volcano sputtering sparks.'

'He is a deep chasm revealing little on the surface.'

'He is a gently flowing river depositing fertile soil on the banks.'

This step develops a more flexible understanding of the other person and awakens a poetic experience, which can lead to greater insight.

Active Talker approach

You can gain further understanding by categorizing the other person. Is he an extrovert? Is he an introvert? What is his temperament? What is his soul attitude?

While metaphor activates images, categorizing draws more strongly on the intellect.

Thinking Organizer approach

What is the other person's biography? What kind of childhood did he have? How has he met life's challenges? What are his goals? His ethics? What motivates him? What are his ideals? What kinds of misunderstandings occur regularly with him? What ways to heal misunderstandings are most successful? What are the joys of spending time with him?

Using this soul quality takes us beyond the sense world to a conscious understanding of the other person.

Spiritual Investigator approach

How does the spirit reveal itself in the other person? How is his life an expression of the divine? What does his life reveal about his higher self? About his higher intentions? How does the work of his 'I' express itself in his deeds? Am I supporting him in recognizing his tasks? How are my deeds affecting his ability to carry out his life's work?

This quality helps us develop a deeper understanding of the being of the other.

Radiant Balancer approach

Can I gain a sense of who this person truly is? How can I behold his higher self? Can I forgive what he has done to me? Can I forgive myself? Can I love this person as a sister or brother?

This quality awakens in us the sense of devotion to the other as well as helping us transform our own personalities.

Using the seven soul gestures as a way of developing understanding of nature

Another way to use the seven soul attitudes is to contemplate nature in a similar way. Whereas our work in contemplating another person tends to be more personal, contemplating nature through these seven steps can lead us to a new relationship with nature and life itself. Both 'ways' can lead us to an experience of pure spirit.

Reflective Preserver approach

We observe how nature provides us with the sun, rain, and earth so that our food will grow. This allows us to see the usefulness of all that is in nature. We can choose a natural object such as a pine cone or we can use the whole of nature as the object of our observation.

This exercise develops objectivity.

Dreamy Nurturer approach

Experience beauty in nature. Beyond the usefulness of nature, we can open ourselves up in awe to its majesty and experience reverence. Every aspect of nature – the beauty of a sunrise, a sunset, dark clouds before a storm, seed leaves appearing in the moist soil, a newborn calf, a spider web – can evoke reverence.

Social Innovator approach

The third step takes us beyond beauty to experiencing every detail of nature as an expression of a spiritual truth. We can see this most clearly through our use of language – when we see how words we use had their origin in nature. When we say that a person is lion-hearted, we use the quality of the lion to indicate courage. Or we say that a person follows a straight path, meaning that he has a direct relationship to a goal and doesn't get distracted. Analogy, simile, and metaphor help us to recognize truths which underlie both nature and the world of human beings. Watching waves, for example, ceaselessly advance on the shore, then retreat, then advance again, our thoughts can turn to the ebb and flow of human relationships and human life.

This activity of the Social Innovator develops flexibility in thinking.

Active Talker approach

The fourth step takes us beyond recognizing that there are relationships between nature and human activity. We discover a lawfulness in what at first seemed coincidence or randomness. Every part of nature offers us lessons through which we categorize and classify. We come to understand intellectual truths. For example, the relationship of minerals, plants, and animals teaches us about environmental interdependency. The need of diversity for a healthy ecosystem can indicate the importance of having diversity in community life. Through nature we learn about the human form and its similarity to other forms in nature. As we experience the unity within nature, we find we are part of it, integral to it.

Discovering lawfulness requires persistence and motivation.

Thinker Organizer approach

Now we use our deepened understanding to penetrate the surfaces of things and come to something beyond the sense world. For example, what is the truth behind interdependency? What picture lies behind the need for diversity in life forms? What is the truth that lives in the form of a spiral in different parts of nature? What is a spiral? What does it express?

Through understanding what we have previously categorized in nature, we can come to Imagination, and a deeper, philosophical experience of truth as embodied in the natural world.

Spiritual Investigator approach

We experience that all of nature is an expression of God. All matter is spirit. Out of this experience, beyond time, the capacity of the Spiritual Investigator takes us into the depths of experience in which we can become aware of the vast possibilities of the human being.

Radiant Balancer approach

Now the grand view lies before us in the seventh step. We must approach the spiritual world through humility and in a new state of consciousness rather than merely through experimentation or intellectual thoughts. We then may experience the unifying elements in nature, the hidden relationships between things and thoughts. No longer limiting ourselves by thinking that man and nature are worlds apart, we now experience them as one and the same. That is, we grasp the world of archetypes. We find that we are not separate from spirit but one with it. To do this, we need to approach nature (and all of life) with love. The light of the Radiant Balancer brings clarity and warmth. 'To see the world in a grain of sand/And heaven in a wild flower' as Blake says. The miraculous is found within the ordinary. The pure idea is freed from the moods and emotions of the soul and allows us to see the world with new eyes.

To sum up

1. Observe physical facts and remember them:
   Reflective Preserver.

2. Develop reverence through experiencing beauty:
   Dreamy Nurturer.

3. Through metaphor, simile, or analogy come to another understanding. 'The seashell is like...', 'The person is like...':
   Social Innovator.

4. Using intellect, categorize, find lawfulness:
   Active Talker.

5. Penetrate beyond the sense world to Imagination:
   Thinker Organizer.

6. Experience that everything is an expression of spirit:
   Spiritual Investigator.

7. Experience unity, the pure idea or archetype:
   Radiant Balancer.

Through these seven steps, the 'I' leads us into an ever-deeper relationship with nature.

Chapter 11. Beyond the Seven Soul Qualities

The seven soul qualities, strongly connected with our personalities, are ours by virtue of who we are, who we were born to be. Each soul quality has its strength and its weakness, and we can choose whether to accentuate its positive side or not. However, there are other attitudes or gestures which are usually associated with older people who have reached a stage of maturity. These attitudes are *universality, compassion,* and *conscience.* Whereas the seven soul qualities are challenges to our soul development, these additional three are qualities of spiritual development. We are completely free to develop them or not.

Universality

This expresses itself in three ways:
(1) in our thinking;
(2) in our feeling;
(3) in our willing.

Universality in our thinking represents a cosmic outlook in our relationship to the entire world. We no longer feel that we are citizens of a particular country only, but rather that we are citizens of all the world and even of the cosmos. No boundary restricts our awareness. We understand the interconnectedness of all aspects of life and incorporate them into our thinking. Thus all of life has meaning and purpose. Albert Einstein said, '... the man who regards his own life and that of his fellow creatures as meaningless is not merely unfortunate but almost disqualified for life.' [1]

When we achieve *universality in our feelings,* we experience true brotherhood. When we meet another human being, we feel humility and reverence. *Universality* in our feelings is grounded in respect, and it expands to evoke a sense of unity and love.

When we achieve *universality in our wills,* our actions are ennobled. We act not only for our own good, but for the good of all. Altruism becomes a natural way of being. I think of former President Jimmie Carter and the many activities he has taken on in his later years – *Habitat for Humanity, Witness for Peace,* and peace emissary in difficult political crises. Mother Theresa also comes quickly to mind in her untiring efforts to care for the poor in India. She described how in each suffering human being she found the Christ.

How can one develop *universality?* It begins with wonder, with cultivating a freshness in seeing the world, so that we meet each day with an eagerness to experience the miracle of life once more.

I have heard it said that 'A person who prays in childhood blesses in old age.' At first, this seemed odd to me. How could prayer in childhood have such an impact decades later? Two experiences have changed my mind. First has been my own experience of growing older. I am amazed at how seemingly unimportant events of my childhood arise in my consciousness and affect my attitude toward the world.

The other experience has been the recent stream of conferences and articles on the significance of the first three years in the child's life. Neurological research shows that love and nurturing during the early years affects brain development, that brains of neglected children do not develop fully, with the result that they will not be able as adults to reach out and nurture the next generation. The gestures which the child experiences are taken into her own soul. The experience of gentleness, caring and reverence calls forth in the child an attitude of nurturing and blessing, whereas anger and violent actions lead to acts of vengeance and abuse when the child becomes an adult.

When we understand the importance of the first three years, we may be able to understand why the child who prays will later have the power to bless. The attitude of those who care for us in our early years works deeply into our soul life. In ways far more mysterious than we can ordinarily understand, we absorb the thoughts and feelings of our caregivers, our parents, relatives and friends. If we have been taught to have reverence for life, for nature, for God, for our parents, other family members and friends, then that reverence or attitude of prayer creates an inner attitude of humility and devotion. It lives in the soul like hidden treasure that we will discover as we mine our inner life for all that lives there, awaiting transformation. Reverence in early childhood naturally transforms into an ability to nurture and bring blessings to others.

A bedtime prayer by Rudolf Steiner embodies such reverence.

> *From my head to my feet,*
> *I am the image of God.*
> *From my heart to my hands,*
> *His own breath do I feel.*
> *When I speak with my mouth*
> *I shall follow God's will,*
> *When I see and know God*
> *In Father and Mother,*
> *In Sister and Brother,*
> *In all loving people,*
> *In the flowers and the trees,*
> *In the birds, beasts, and stones.*
> *Then no fear shall I feel.*
> *Only love will then fill me*
> *For all that is around me.*[2]

What about those of us who didn't have this attitude in childhood? Will we be able to achieve an attitude of reverence, to be able to bless those around us? We human beings are amazingly resilient. To some degree we can compensate through our own efforts for what we may have missed. If we did not have a sense of reverence instilled in us as children, we can still cultivate a sense of devotion as adults, even though our path may be harder and more uphill. We can transform our soul life so that we can experience universality in our thinking, feeling, and will. We can transform our thinking so that it becomes clear and objective, awakening in us an understanding of the connectedness of life. We can purify our desires so that we become unselfish, and we can transform our will so that we gladly assume responsibility for others as well as ourselves. When we acknowledge the spiritual nature of our 'I' and the power of our 'I' to create ourselves, we are on the road to developing universality in our later years. What we did in earlier periods of life – whether we acted courageously and for the good of others, whether we looked out beyond ourselves, whether we developed self-discipline, patience, and stability – will build a foundation for us to act with humility, reverence, and love.

Another way of saying this is that we can incorporate the positive aspects of the Active Talker, the Thinker Organizer, and the Spiritual Investigator to establish a foundation on which to build.

Compassion

The attitude of *compassion* takes us beyond our thoughts into our emotional life. In our middle years we tend to focus on proving and promoting ourselves. Except for family members, concern for others is not usually our main focus. As we establish our own individuality and come to peace with who we are, we are better able to reach out, to empathize, and to feel compassion for others.

The soul qualities of the Dreamy Nurturer and of the Social Innovator are transformed into the ability to perceive the needs of others and to try to meet them.

Conscience

The third attitude is *conscience*. Whereas compassion leads from the soul outward into the world, *conscience* relates inwardly. We become an inner judge of our own actions, examining our lives, setting things right, making peace where there was conflict.

When we were children, we achieved the three great accomplishments of being human: we learned to walk, to speak and to think. In our later years, we can raise these physical deeds to a moral level. Just as we once learned to walk upright, to place one foot in front of the other, which eventually enabled us to skip, hop, and jump, in our later years we can choose to be upright morally. Through examining our consciences and choosing to do the good, we can move through life purposefully and consciously.

Just as through learning to speak we entered the world of language, developing means of communicating our feelings, our needs, our thoughts, so as mature adults we can use our speech to heal, to comfort, to reconcile, to affirm others. Through speech we can impart wisdom learned from life's lessons.

As children we learned to think, to consider, to contrast, to be logical, to understand the world. With the power of thinking we could penetrate its laws and master the world. So, as mature adults, we can transform our thinking into deeper understanding of the effect of thoughts, developing inner perception of the effects of our thoughts on our actions.

All religious teachings have given rules of behavior, of how to act toward one's neighbors, oneself, and toward the spiritual world. That is necessary for an orderly society. Living by rules regulates and orders society. However, true conscience awakens from an inner source, from inner experience.

Conscience is our inner corrector. It is far more important to have a clear conscience than to have material wealth.

Through developing aspects of *universality, compassion,* and *conscience* we can be more inwardly tranquil and a blessing to others.

SECTION III

TWELVE WINDOWS INTO THE WORLD

The archetypes

One of the tasks of later adolescence is to use thinking as a way of bringing light to the emotional life and modifying it. In adulthood, thinking becomes a mode of relating to the world which develops particular viewpoints. These can be philosophical viewpoints such as materialism or skepticism; or ones which accept the existence of a spiritual world. Another way to look at it is to see that such viewpoints can relate to the archetypes which exist as part of the human journey. In other words, a person can approach life from the point of view of a warrior or of an orphan (usually seen as being a victim). The viewpoint is strongly influenced by earlier life experiences, but it is also open to change. It is much more accessible than the temperament or even the soul attitude because it can be influenced by our 'I'. Our 'I' can consciously rethink our life, realizing that certain situations were responsible for our point of view, and therefore with new information we can develop a new viewpoint. Joseph Campbell did a great deal to bring archetypes from mythology to our awareness. His lifework, especially his book **The Hero with a Thousand Faces**,[1] has contributed mythological archetypes to our general psychological language.

The philosophical viewpoints, as well as archetypes, have often been related to the twelve Zodiacal signs. In co-teaching the medieval epic **Parsifal** with my colleague Brian Gray, we have found that when I present the twelve archetypal stages of the journey this fits in beautifully with his presentations of the zodiacal qualities of the chapters.

Within the twelve archetypes – the Innocent, the Orphan, the Warrior, the Caregiver, the Seeker, the Destroyer, the Lover, the Creator, the Ruler, the Healer, the Sage, and the Fool – one can see that some relate more to will (e.g. the Warrior), some more to feelings (e.g. the Caregiver), and some to thinking (e.g. the Sage.) However, all these have a thinking quality to them, just as the Soul attitudes all have a feeling quality.

A person may have a Choleric temperament, a Dreamy Nurturer soul quality, and approach life through the viewpoint of a Healer. The Choleric temperament makes a person forceful, strong, and dominant. The Dreamy Nurturer soul quality enables the Choleric to use this strength to care for others. By approaching life from the viewpoint of a Healer, he can use his strength and caring tendencies to heal or bring transformation to others or to himself.

Another person may have a Melancholic temperament, a Thinker-Organizer soul quality, and may approach life from the viewpoint of a Destroyer. This Melancholic person might be one who sees life as a glass half-empty, worried about many things. However, his Thinker-Organizer soul quality lifts the Melancholic temperament to a broad overview so that he can realize that there are patterns in life that he can learn to understand. He can use his Melancholic temperament to bring sensitivity to his planning and organizing. From the Destroyer viewpoint he can see the importance of letting parts of his life die so they can be transformed into something new.

The combination of temperament, soul quality, and archetypal viewpoint offer us at least three ways to understand aspects of our soul life.

Chapter 1. Experiencing Twelve Archetypes Within

In her book, *Spirit Quest: The Initiation of an Indian Boy*,[2] Carol Batdorf quotes the words of a Native American elder.

> 'There are many kinds of men,' he said after a long silence. 'Some are born to action – to fight, to strive, to make themselves heard. Others are born to think, to feel, to reason. Each is a leader in his own way. My son, the secret of it – the magic of it – is to know which way is your way. Do not strive to be that which you are not. If you are to be a warrior and a leader like your father, then be it. Search for the spirit gifts which will make you a great warrior and a wise and true leader of men. But if your mind lies in another direction, do not hesitate to take that way. Then you must search for power that will help you – not to be a leader of men, but one who works through another calling. A great canoe-maker is truly a person of value. One, like myself, who can heal and advise is also important. So it is. But whatever path you walk, work with every gift you have to be the best that it is in you to be. That is our way.'

In addition to the seven soul qualities presented in the previous section, I will describe twelve archetypes. Each represents a path toward the realization of the Self or the 'I'. On this path there are possibilities for self-development which the individual can freely choose to engage in or not.

Development of each of the twelve archetypes

1. The Innocent

The Innocent starts life by naively trusting everyone. She expects to be cared for and nurtured and likes to lean on others. As Innocents encounter unfairness or violence, the illusion of Paradise may be shattered, and they reflect their disappointment by blaming others for their own mistakes. They are quick to see other people's faults and to feel sorry for themselves. However, the Innocent needs to gain balance, to accept contradictions without losing faith that there is goodness in the world.

When they do gain their balance, they have the strength that comes with optimism, the assumption that life can be better. Out of this balance, the Innocent develops perspective on life. Confidence and optimism carry Innocents through struggles until they gain wisdom. Innocents who have matured carry their optimism into adult life, which helps them to reach higher levels of goodness, transforming youthful idealism into mature idealism.

Innocents who have not matured limit their possibilities for growth. They often have difficulty growing up. They long to return to the innocence of childhood and expect perfection in those around them. They want to recapture the care and love of childhood, so they crave acceptance and approval from others. Because Innocents want to be safe, they look for protectors. They often harbor fears which prevent them from dealing with hurt and pain in a mature way. Some Innocents refuse to change and are unable to accept themselves, to forgive themselves, or let go of their immature identities. At any age an Innocent may recognize that she is carrying this early archetype inappropriately. It's never too late to work these problems through and come to a new level of maturity.

2. The Orphan

The Orphan has lost the childlike sense of being protected and feels all alone, with no one there to help. When problems arise, the Orphan often feels like a helpless victim and looks for someone to solve the problem or rescue her. At the same time, however, she doesn't really expect help. This ambivalence may lead to one of two results: either she covers up her weakness or fear with a hard shell of cynicism, or she appears overly vulnerable and open to being manipulated by others.

Orphans live with contradictory feelings. The Orphan wants to be helped, but doesn't expect to be helped. When she is able to face her situation and recognize the pain of it, she can gain strength over her powerlessness. A big step comes when she is able to speak about her pain and share her fears. Admitting helplessness is very difficult for the Orphan, since she has been protecting herself from showing her true feelings for so long. She has to realize that she needs help and be willing to ask for it. If she can develop a few close relationships with friends she can trust, she may be able to open her heart and share herself. Out of this awareness, the Orphan can learn appropriate dependence in which she relates to others. She then can come to recognize that she is not a helpless victim, that she has power and strength.

The adult who has not been able to transform her Orphan archetype often uses her feeling of being a victim as a way of manipulating those around her. She enjoys getting others to feel sorry for her. She can be very cynical and caustic, even cruel in her treatment of others. Some Orphans continue to feel cast-out, rejected and ostracized. As they experience their own isolation, they may rebel against authority. They may brood or they may attack. The danger of the Orphan archetype is a lack of inner strength. Orphans want approval so badly that they are susceptible to group pressure; they are followers who will carry out orders because they want to feel needed. They also harbor such resentment against people in their own lives that they can project this onto others in a cruel manner.

Transformation of the Orphan is difficult. We see Orphans in juvenile detention centres and prisons: lonely, miserable, self-destructive human beings who desperately want to love but who trust no one. We meet Orphans in the workplace as people who can't understand why life deals them so many hard knocks. They don't understand that they are helping to create the situation by blaming others for their problems. The longer they put off examining why they continually meet problems, the longer it will take them to transform themselves. Transformation of the Orphan comes through trusting others. The arts can be especially helpful in this process, as they awaken a sense of power, on one hand, and wonder, on the other. Success, however, will depend on the depth of the artistic experience. Orphans often fool themselves by approaching problems superficially. With much effort and deep inner work, the Orphan can awaken to self-worth as well as to the realization that it's time to let go of the past and concentrate on the future.

3. The Warrior

The Warrior looks at life as a competition, a contest in which one wins or loses. When a problem arises, it must be taken hold of and overcome. The enemy must be defeated. This aggressive stance is characteristic of the Warrior, who can't bear feeling weak or power-less. She musters her energies to confront the challenge or overcome the obstacle, to fight for the right. The positive aspect of this approach is that Warriors develop discipline and courage. They are willing to face demons and conquer them, to expose themselves to danger, determined to triumph over evil.

In the early stage, Warriors are simply fighters. The Warrior fights to defend herself or those whom she protects. She doesn't clearly distinguish between worthy and unworthy causes; she simply defines the other as bad and tries to destroy him or her. As the Warrior matures, however, she finds a reason for her fighting. She convinces herself that she is fighting for a principle or for another person. She doesn't wish to destroy the other, only to achieve her goal in a positive manner – but if that means a fight, so be it. She does not choose violence; she just wants things to work out for the best for everyone. Yet she cannot ignore a challenge and would never forgive herself if she didn't step forward and fight.

Unless the Warrior goes through a transformative process, she takes everything personally and is easily insulted. Her temper flares, she feels singled out for humiliation. She cannot bear it if someone disagrees with her, and she does not like losing arguments. She is so fixed on winning that she may behave rudely and crudely, defeating the enemy with relish. She cannot compromise because her honor is at stake. She is constantly trying to prove herself because inwardly she does not feel worthy. Therefore she wants to be the biggest and the best, seeking high status and power to show that she really is 'somebody'. Untransformed Warriors can be frightening people, quick to flare, unpredictable, always ready to impose themselves on others. Transformed, however, they become people who are willing to stand up and fight for their principles while being able to listen to those whose ideas are different. They are admired for their commitment and respected for their balanced approach.

Gradually the maturing Warrior awakens to the question: Where does all this aggression come from? Is the enemy within or without? How can I honestly and effectively solve the problem? As the Warrior matures, she gains capacities of high leadership and brings strength and vision to a group or community. Because of her persistence and dedication to a cause, she 'carries the banner' and stays with it until she has accomplished what she needs to.

The Warrior archetype is the prevalent mode of being in Western society. This puts stress on the other archetypes because so much in our society is seen in terms of competition, of winners and losers, of fighting and vanquishing. Examples in our language that express the warrior archetype are such sayings as 'Level the playing field', 'Politics is a game', 'Play the game (work the system)', 'Kill time' and 'crushing victory'.

4. The Caregiver

Caregivers are very different from Warriors. Rather than trying to fight her way through life, the Caregiver's main intention is to help others. She wants things to work out, to have peace. She will give herself totally to helping others. If there is a problem, she wants to solve it. If a person is hurt, physically or emotionally, she wants to heal or cure. She wants to console, nurture, affirm. Her goal is to help others through love and sacrifice.

She can't bear the thought of being considered selfish, because everything about her bespeaks unselfishness. She reaches out with compassion for those in need; she will give away her material goods, her money, her heart. She will go out of her way to create situations in which the other person will feel accepted, recognized, nurtured.

Caregivers put out extra effort to help others who belong to the group. They start conversations, they invite people to their homes, they call on the telephone, they bring over a meal, they think of all the nice things that can brighten a day. When a stranger enters the group, the Caregiver goes right over and welcomes the newcomer, extending warmth and friendship.

As with other archetypes, Caregivers can go too far and actually have a negative influence on others as well as on themselves. The immature Caregiver is unable to distinguish how much of herself to give, so she gives her all – and has nothing left. When asked for help, the Caregiver doesn't know how to say 'no'.

Often Caregivers are taken advantage of. Or they may barge in uninvited and try to care for a person who doesn't want to be cared for. This gesture is experienced as smothering, especially if the Caregiver is compulsive about it. Some Caregivers expect to be treated the same way in return and resent it when others don't come to help *them* in their need, seeing themselves as martyrs. 'No one ever cares about me. I do everything for everyone else. All right, I'll just have to exhaust myself helping others without any recognition.' Caregivers need to respect themselves and know when too much is being asked of them. They have to pay as much attention to their own need for balance and health as they pay to the needs of others.

Another example of the immature Caregiver is the person who gives a gift or does something for someone else but with expectations attached to it.

'Yes, you can go on a vacation, but you should know that I'll be exhausted from taking on all your responsibility. It's fine. Just go and have a good time. I don't mind.'

'I'm giving you money to buy a car, but I want to be sure you buy one which I approve of.'

'You need a new table. I'll go with you to choose the right one.'

Such remarks make us wonder whether we really want to accept the gift. These are the remarks of Caregivers who have not transformed their sense of generosity and need to control situations.

Then there is the Caregiver who walks around feeling guilty all the time. Such Caregivers become victims of their own weakness. They want to help other people so much that they feel that they are to blame for other people's problems.

Other Caregivers have such a need to be needed that they excuse inappropriate behavior in their friends, partners, or children. What is needed is a firm but loving hand. Such people end up repeatedly having relationships with those who struggle with alcohol or drug addiction. They are sensitive to the addict's hard life or other circumstances leading to the addiction, but each time they excuse the addict's behavior, they help her avoid dealing with the problem.

The immature Caregiver can hardly resist the call of someone in need. Over and over, she excuses her inability to meet her own responsibilities because she had to help someone else. A needy person always know that the Caregiver will bend over backward to be kind and loving, so an unhealthy relationship of mutual dependence can develop between the two.

As Caregivers mature, they learn to distinguish strengths from weaknesses. At first, the Caregiver feels a general need to 'care' and doesn't distinguish her own needs from those of others. She will give everything for the other person, no matter the price. She is always looking for someone who is weaker, someone to take care of, because her own sense of self-worth is identified with this role. Slowly, the Caregiver realizes that she also has to care for herself, that she is not actually helping the other person by enabling her to perpetuate her weakness. She sees that sometimes she must hold back and not rush in to take care of the other person. Then the other can begin to grow up and take care of herself. As Caregivers become inwardly stronger and no longer rely on the satisfaction of being needed, they become clearer in their own minds as to when help is appropriate.

Then the Caregiver moves on to the third stage. Now she can care for people, for animals, for the planet by appropriately fighting for causes, participating in clean-up days, volunteering in convalescent homes, delivering 'meals-on-wheels', calling Neighborhood Watch meetings, and in many other ways. Without sacrificing her own sense of balance, she contributes to the community in a wonderful way.

Caregivers often go into the caring professions, such as nursing, teaching, and social work. Unfortunately, our society shows greater appreciation and recognition for Warrior types, while Caregiver professions and occupations are often underpaid and unrecognized.

5. The Seeker

'The young man left home and went out to seek his fortune', says the Fairy Tale.

The Seeker path is a major theme of fairy tales and legends from many lands. Seekers express themselves in many forms but the common element is that they are always searching for a better life or a higher truth. How many people today leave their everyday lives and go off 'to find themselves' – to see the world, to travel or study, to explore different styles of living, to find spiritual meaning! Afraid of becoming trapped in traditions and customs, they take off in search of something different, something more fulfilling than they previously had.

The immature Seeker wants the answers now! When she doesn't find what she is looking for, she leaves. She doesn't stay around. She escapes. She is searching for Utopia. Longing for perfection, she nostalgically yearns to return to childhood, to a happier time. The Search is especially attractive to us in our twenties, when we are looking for our life's path.

Later, in midlife, we again search, no longer satisfied with the choices we made earlier or the material possessions we have accumulated. Again we are restless, feeling unfulfilled. Often we have made compromises along the way, forsaking the dreams and ideals of our youth. As we try to reconnect with what we have lost, we again become Seekers. We break with the old – or sometimes the old breaks with us, as when a spouse leaves.

In the next stage in the Seeker's development, she does not try to escape responsibility but embraces it. She seeks something higher than her own satisfaction to give meaning to life. As we look for meaning we are constantly faced with the issue of truth. Our search for truth grows more persistent as we mature, even though it may bring pain and suffering.

6. Destroyer

Destroyers deal with endings – of things, of phases, of life. Immature Destroyers are confused and angry over losing something or someone. They are hurt and try to deny that something death-like is happening. To cover up fear, the Destroyer may destroy another person or herself through bad habits, carelessness, or neglect.

Feeling powerless, the Destroyer desperately tries to gain a sense of power by manipulating others or by using substances to mask her feeling of despair. When the Destroyer experiences a threat, she feels that she must destroy the problem or be destroyed by it.

The next stage comes when the Destroyer accepts the inevitability of death, recognizes that we are all mortal, that in one way or another we are all powerless and need the help of a higher power. This change requires the Destroyer to face her pain, to acknowledge that she is lonely, that she needs others, to be willing to change. Facing her worst fears helps the Destroyer let go of burdens she has carried for a long time. Letting go allows the Destroyer to experience love for the first time.

A person may become a Destroyer after a traumatic experience. For example, her child may have been killed in an automobile accident, or her spouse or parent harmed. She feels bitter, angry and helpless as she absorbs the loss and injustice. The experience may plunge her into feeling that this tragedy would not have happened if life had any meaning.

A Destroyer advances to a mature level when she learns to accept and let go. She realizes that she must change, that she cannot go on as she has been, for she is harming herself. She needs to give up the past without denying her pain and suffering. Shedding her anger and grief allows the Destroyer's transformation to begin. She will have to let go of all her coping techniques and accept her vulnerability. When this happens, the Destroyer becomes open to new realities. If she accepts the need to undergo transformation, she is then willing to sacrifice her old self for the new. In this way she is freed from her old identity.

We all experience the Destroyer archetype because we must all face death. We can deny it for a long time, but at some point we must admit to ourselves that we too will die. It is only a matter of when. We cannot bargain with God, and accepting our mortality is a part of becoming a mature human being. When we do accept death, new possibilities arise.

For example, composer Gustav Mahler was an active, energetic man, always busy – whether composing, carrying out administrative tasks, bicycling or hiking in the Austrian countryside. During the summer of 1907, Mahler, known for his aggressive, impatient, demanding, and turbulent manner, was confronted by three terrible situations – his daughter died, he left the Vienna Opera after ten years, and he learned that he had a severe heart condition.

At first, he went into deep depression. Then, in place of his usual difficult manner, new qualities emerged. He became sweeter, more patient, and contemplative. In a letter to Bruno Walter, he wrote, 'At the end of my life I must go back to living like a beginner and learn again how to stand.' He told Walter that he had to 'find his way again and overcome the terrors of loneliness.'³ His newly achieved meditative gesture toward life led him to a deeper, more sensitive appreciation of nature, of destiny, and of life itself. Out of these reflections, he composed, during the closing months of his life, the symphonic celebration, *The Song of the Earth*, his farewell to and celebration of the earth.

Mahler incorporated Chinese poems in the lyrics of the symphony and added to them these lines of his own: *Still ist mein Herz und harret seiner Stunde. Die liebe Erde allüberall blüht auf im Lenz und grünt aufs neu.* ('My heart is peaceful, awaiting its hour. The beloved earth everywhere flowers and is green again.') His work lives on as a great testimony to the human spirit. In Mahler, the Destroyer archetype had been transformed. Facing pain, he experienced joy. Facing ignorance, he gained wisdom. Facing loneliness, he experienced love.

7. The Lover

On the most primitive level, the Lover lives in sympathy and antipathy, drawn to what she instinctively loves or hates. In one extreme form, she become easily infatuated, seduced, and overcome with emotion. In the other extreme, the Lover reacts by fearfully holding back from love, choosing instead extreme asceticism. She denies herself the experience, punishing herself, while at the same time yearning for love.

The Lover is impulsive and fickle, blown this way and that by passion's pull. Swimming in the ecstasy of love, Lovers take refuge in bliss and do not want to leave it or lose it. If their love is threatened, they try to hold on to what they have, attaching themselves to the beloved, unable to give up the relationship. They like the thrill of being in love. However, if they feel in the slightest that their love is threatened, they react with jealous rages, obsessive aggression and possessiveness. Many violent acts are committed in impulsive fits of jealousy.

An important step is made when Lovers move beyond the sensual and feel love of companionship, of shared experiences, of deep friendship, of committed relationship. Rather than running away or finding a new object to love every time they lose the ecstatic feeling, the more mature Lover realizes that a deeper level of love is growing. She realizes that she must lose the earlier kind of love in order to come to something richer and longer lasting. At this stage if she feels that her love is threatened, she tries to overcome jealousy and grasp what is happening, and what can be done to heal the relationship.

The even more mature Lover is capable of still greater depth of feeling and understanding. When the Lover goes beyond the personal element, she makes contact with people who are different, people who do not at first seem lovable. From the transformation of personal instinctive love emerge the qualities of compassion, forgiveness, and understanding. As Lovers move from one stage to another, they go from *Eros*, sensual love, to *Philos*, love of friends, or love of the other as brother or sister, to *Caritas*, love of others (from which we get the word 'charity'); and finally to *Agape*, spiritual love.

All of us experience the Lover archetype in ourselves as our relationships go beyond the infatuation stage.

8. The Creator

The Creator looks at the world as an opportunity to create, to make something new, to respond to problems in an imaginative way. In the first stage, the Creator loves to dream, to lose herself in fantasy, to try new ways without seeing them through. In the second stage, she focuses more strongly, sees what needs to be done, and sets about doing it. She takes hold of life and applies her energies to creating change where it is needed.

By the third stage, the Creator has proven capable of bringing about change in a mature way. Skillfully she takes hold of opportunities and creates new solutions. The more skillful she becomes, the more risks she is willing to take. She feels secure enough to create a new vision for her life, which allows her to do what she always has dreamed of doing.

The archetypal Creator is the one who gives birth – to children, to art, to inventions, to the universe itself. The Creator is represented by God, gods and goddesses of the ancient world, the earth, fathers, mothers, artists, inventors, and visionaries of all kinds. Of course, Creators also include novelists, dramatists, poets, painters, sculptors, photographers, musicians, and craftspeople. What they have in common with other Creators is that they can see the extraordinary within the ordinary, and are able to bring about new relationships, new combinations, new visions. They use tools, they shape materials, they step onto new ground, and they dare to dream what has not been realized previously. They reflect on their activities, and at the end of the process, they can say, 'It is Good'.

Creators in the business world create a broad vision of the goals and challenges facing their companies. They see where the company is heading in five years, in ten years, what changes will have to be made, what new products will need to be designed, and what new management styles will need to be implemented.

Teachers who are Creators see each class as a symphony or a palette of living colors. They are midwives whose task it is to bring to birth the potential that lives within the children, to design and carry out programs that stimulate and awaken children's interest.

Scientists who are Creators see new ways of doing things, new inventions, new arrangements of substance, and they see new patterns in what is seemingly chaotic. They are able to develop new tools, new machines, new medicines, new ways of working with landforms.

The Creator's need to create is so strong she may prefer to live in poverty as long as she can serve her craft, her muse. It drives her, but she cannot change herself. In addition to focusing on the outer tasks, Creators also turn their activity inward. They become co-creators with the spiritual world, shaping their dreams, shaping their possibilities, and shaping their relationships. As creators, they form, mould, transform, innovate, and conceive. As they create their dreams and their possibilities, they also accept themselves. They create identities which express their picture of who they are. Creators are generally optimists who approach the world with positive and creative energy. They say, Why not? Let's try. This may be possible!

The Creator who turns her vision inward is able to create the broad picture of her life. She sees life itself as an art form, much as Mary Catherine Bateson expresses in the title of her book, *Composing a Life: Life as a Work in Progress.*[4] As the dustjacket states, 'Bateson's life-affirming conclusion is that life is an improvisational art form, and that the interruptions, conflicted priorities, and exigencies that are a part of all our lives can, and should, be seen as a source of wisdom.' When Creators approach life in this way, they take responsibility for their lives. This is in sharp contrast to those who see themselves as victims of an unseen enemy. A Creator hears the footsteps of destiny moving through the pattern of her life.

A wonderful description of the archetypal Creator is found in the journals of Bronson Alcott, 19th century New England philosopher and educator.

> Spirit! 'Tis the architect of nature. It builds her temples. It moulds her bodies. Life is its work. It clothes itself in Nature then anon it casts aside its robes … Forms vanish. The arch of nature gives way. There is no footway across the stream of Time. Then again, Spirit rebuilds the bridge, and the terrestrial sojourner proceeds on his way to the bourne of immortality.[5]

The Creator archetype also has a negative side. Those Creators who approach the world pessimistically see the downside of everything and sometimes are paralyzed by it. They see what is not possible, limits rather than opportunity. Their impulse is to create, but they are constantly hampered by self-doubt, which limits them and weakens or even blocks their creative impulses. They may try incessantly to produce, but obstacle after obstacle stymies them. Other immature creators restlessly produce work after work without taking time to fully develop their creations. They compulsively begin new projects even though existing projects are still rough or incomplete. Action for its own sake takes hold of them. They are under the one-sided sway of their archetype.

The Creator swings between one pole, which promises expansion, breaking of limits, and freedom; and another pole, of obstruction, suffering, and being bound by limits. On one side is the angel winging into the heavens, unbound by earthly limitations, becoming one with God the Creator. On the other is the demon, possessed, barren, frustrated, and doubting.

The challenge for the mature Creator is to hold on to her passionately inspired imagination, while she practices, drills, and prepares the skills needed to accomplish her grand vision. Sweat and toil are part of the Creator's process as much as the sweetness of inspiration. Consider the birth pains which a mother endures before that moment of elation when the child's head crowns and a new soul is born into the world. Tears and laughter often inter-mingle at the moment of creation.

Creators carry some of the wonder and innocence of a child into their adult lives. Children are spontaneous and unselfconscious. Creators, too, must find these qualities within themselves and awaken child-like perception and joy. No one is ever too old to create – a beautiful phrase, a letter of love, a tender word, a dish of steaming stir-fry, a garden of voluptuous blooms, a hand-knit sweater, a moment of joy, a warm handshake, a smile. In every moment of our lives we can be Creators.

9. The Ruler

Each of us has to bring order into his or her life and thus we express the Ruler archetype that lives within us. How we bring order depends on the kind of ruler we are. We live in many different relationships – to our mates, our families, our co-workers or colleagues, our neighborhoods, and so on. Each of these situations calls on us to take responsibility, to direct our activities to accomplish our goals.

In order to decide what kind of Ruler we will be, we need to define our goals. What do we want our children to grow up to be, what is the aim of our work, what mood do we want to have in our job, what do we expect of ourselves? Closely linked to being a ruler is the role of authority. We can be the tyrant, the demagogue, the master; we can be the sharer, the supporter, the encourager; we can take credit for success, we can place the credit on others.

At the first stage, the Ruler takes charge of those situations closest to her. She makes sure that the family survives, that work-goals are achieved, that life's daily problems are solved. She is motivated to do a good job and to fulfill the expectations which her family and employer have of her She tries to rule her own life in a similar way, by being a disciplined, responsible person.

The second stage Ruler feels confidence in the security of her family and job. Now she can turn her energy in two directions – she can contribute her skills to the community, to the church, the neighborhood, the town where she has a direct connection, and she can use her strength to develop her inner life so that she grows more effective, more competent in whatever she chooses to do.

In the third stage, the Ruler goes much further afield. She uses her well-developed skills for those whom she doesn't know – for the country, for other nations around the world, for the earth, for children, for literacy, for the homeless, for the ill and the aged.

We all have to be Rulers in some part of our lives. When we rule with wisdom, we feel independence and freedom. We feel competent and responsible. At other times, we become either too bossy or ineffective, so that disorder and chaos follows. Then we are not effective. Rulers swing between the extremes of control and lack of control.

When Rulers have too strong control over others, they dominate, smother, victimize, and arrogantly and egotistically control every-one's life. They are sure that they have the only right answers. They manipulate to get their own way. They make others feel inept, weak, resentful, and dependent. Weak Rulers, on the other hand, are wishy-washy, unable to focus on the problem at hand, resented, pitied, not respected or admired. They make people feel frustrated, nervous, worried, and willing to take risks to change the situation.

Between the two extremes are Rulers who try to gauge problems clearly and effectively. Their concern is to respond in a constructive manner, to accomplish the goals at hand, and to support the efforts of everyone involved. They seek to bring harmony. They work for the greater good.

We see weak rulers in parents who are not able to bring form to their family life. They cannot manage their households, support their children effectively, help them solve their problems, set boundaries, or aim for goals.

Other parents bring so much form to family life that the atmosphere is stifling. They manage the household like an army barrack, set unrealistic goals, put extreme pressure on their children, make all the decisions for their children, and stifle their imagination and maturation by holding them down.

Rulers of countries can have similar extremes. However, an effective Ruler lives in the tension between too much control and too little, as she ensures that society protects its citizens at the same time as respecting their rights and freedom.

The key element for the archetype of the Ruler is power. As Rulers of our own lives, we also have to consider the way we use power. Do we assume the power we should, or are we too passive? Do we take responsibility for ourselves rather than blaming others? Where does our power come from? Are there times when power by itself is not appropriate? We may need to use other forms of relating. Sometimes restraint is called for. Learning to compromise rather than becoming stubbornly unyielding is part of becoming the mature ruler.

Unlike the Creator, the Ruler does not take time to dream dreams. The Ruler has to exert responsibility in all situations.

When do we become rulers? We see a task at hand, something that needs doing, chaos that needs ordering. We may decide that we have been playing around, and it is time to take responsibility for our lives. We may examine our life and decide we need to take it in hand. Perhaps it is time to learn certain skills, get a good job, make a decent wage. Or it may be time to become clear about the principles which guide us.

There are many exercises on the path to self-mastery, becoming the rulers of ourselves. Most of these have in common the strengthening of the 'I', so that the individual can stand firmly on the ground, with clarity and purpose, making decisions and directing her will to accomplish the task at hand.

10. The Healer

The archetype Healer is also referred to as Magician or Transformer. The Healer is particularly skillful at transformation, using her power to bring about healing, wholeness, new insight, and new possibilities. We can probably call to mind people who exude strength and good will. We enjoy being around them because they bring out our best possible side. We feel stronger and more capable when we are with them. Such people don't have to say much. They are themselves. These people are Healers. In the first stage, the Healer becomes dimly conscious that she has a capacity which others don't. Although each of us has some aspect of the Healer archetype, some people have it more strongly. Any of us may at some time sense that a friend is becoming ill or family members are becoming alienated from each other. We may have a 'sixth sense' that something is going to happen.

After completing my teacher training in England, I spent a year working with emotionally disturbed children. I found that working with those children sensitized my perceptions so that when I later worked with 'normal' children, I could spot tendencies before they developed into major disorders. Mothers often have a similar sensitivity in that they can tell when a child is becoming ill, even before symptoms manifest. When one asks how they know, they can't give a rational explanation. They simply know. Some people have extrasensory perception. They see or hear what is not visible to others.

The main point about the first stage is that the capacity for healing is in the area of perception. The person is not yet sure about what is being perceived, but is prepared to watch more carefully. When other people question the perception, make fun of it, or deny it, the Healer in the first stage may lose confidence in the perception and try to cover it up. This can hinder the development of an important capacity. Someone else may say, in a derogatory way, 'That's just a figment of your imagination', 'You must be seeing things', or 'Are you some kind of witch or something?' When a person feels that her intuition is right and not something to be laughed at or ignored, she is awakening to the Healer archetype. Often the person has to protect the experience by not speaking about it.

Rudolf Steiner described that he had had such an experience at the age of nine, when the figure of a woman appeared to him and beckoned.[6] When he returned home, he learned that a relative had died at exactly that moment. He had other experiences of this nature, but for years he did not speak of them. He found no one in his circle of friends who would acknowledge the possibility of such events. Lonely, he kept his inner experiences to himself for over twenty years. When Steiner finally did speak out, he alienated some of his materialistic admirers who could not accept that he claimed to have had supersensible experiences, which could not be proven empirically.

In the second stage, Healers not only sense that something is happening, they act on their intuitions. For example, some people are very good at finding objects which others have misplaced. They can visualize the lost object and then go right to the spot where it is. Some people sense warmth coming from an object, even though this warmth is not thermally measurable. Some recognize that they have special powers. Some can heal through touch, others through the power of the word.

Some Healers make a particular contribution to a group. When they are not around or not involved, situations may become sticky and knotted. When they take hold of a problem, however, their impulse is to heal it or transform the problem so that it gets resolved.

The Stage Three Healer becomes adept at using knowledge of the interrelationships of all things. She realizes that to make changes in the physical sphere, she first must change the way people think, feel, and relate to the spiritual world. She consciously works to awaken people's understanding and insight into things seen and unseen.

As with all the archetypes, the Healer can have a negative side. When she misuses her powers, she can cause harm. Even in our daily lives, we notice that some people are especially able to influence others. On one level, they are merely charismatic, but they can go too far, using their charisma to exploit people.

The quality of the Healer archetype is expressed in our daily lives in many ways. When we perceive a situation and understand what needs to happen, but we don't force it, we are using this capacity in ourselves. A Warrior would force the 'right' solution to achieve the goal. The Healer watches the process carefully and quietly, supporting what has to happen so that something new can arise.

We can turn the Healer's gaze upon ourselves. By watching carefully how particular events relate to other events, or how at a particular moment certain people appear in our lives, how we come to the right place at the right time, we can perhaps see the hand of destiny at work. In fairy tales, the hero is often is guided by an animal or old woman or old man. These frequently act as Healers, using enchantment as a way of orchestrating the plot.

The presence of the Healer in ourselves is often experienced in connection with names. For instance, in ancient times, this recognition of special powers was often embodied in a person's name. Among Native Americans, for example, a baby was named by tribal elders according to the power that was seen to be working through her. Such names as Stormcloud or Mountain Lion, Running Wind or Starcatcher, were given because the child carried a power related to that aspect of nature.

In the Old Testament, Adam's naming of the animals showed that he could see into the power and gesture of each animal and pronounce the name which was right for it. In many cultures, the mother or father dreams the child's name before she is born.

It is not only ancient names which have power, however. A woman who for many years had felt powerless learned one day that she had been adopted and that she was not carrying the name that had been given her at birth. Through a complicated process, she discovered her true name. When she said it, a tingling went through her body. She had found her power and was able to feel new strength and purpose.

It is not unusual for a person to feel that her given name doesn't fit. Such people often choose to be known by their middle name or a nickname, while some create a new name. Only then do they feel that they can be themselves. I once participated in a naming ceremony for an adult who was choosing her 'true name'. For her, the ceremony was as powerful a spiritual activity as a baptism.

I have heard African-Americans describe how powerless and inferior they felt when they were addressed as 'Boy' rather than by name. When a person is called by name, it is a sign of respect and acknowledgment.

When a person has her right name, she meets the world in a confident assertive way, inwardly at peace. This peace radiates into the environment and other people can sense our inner poise and contentment.

The Healer is comfortable crossing thresholds, such as those between wakefulness and sleep, between death and rebirth, between physical world and spirit world. The Healer is the wise one who understands the laws. In legends, the Healer sometimes changes shape to bring about change. In the medieval story of Parzival, for instance, Cundrie the sorceress becomes an ugly-looking monster who pronounces the truth that no one wants to hear. Her actions cause the hero to take a different path, one which is truer to his true life's quest. In our daily lives, we see this when someone says something to us which wakes us up and causes us to rethink what we are doing.

When we connect ourselves to the spiritual world, we are usually working in the realm of the Healer. When we enter into conscious work, we are embarking on a transformative process.

We can find the Healer archetype expressed in our lives by reflecting on magical moments – on those rituals that created new states of being. The Healer is at work when a boy becomes a man through a rite of passage, when we marry and create a new community, when we experience the miracle of bearing a child. Any time we feel that we have changed because of an experience, we are in touch with the Healer.

The Healer can work on several levels. The transformative process in everyday life brings about new ways of doing things, of transforming negative situations into positive. The Healer can also work on a subtler level, i.e. on a supersensible plane. I feel that there is enough evidence to acknowledge that these experiences really exist.

11. The Sage

The Sage is the wise person who understands on many levels. Often quiet, often humble, the Sage seeks the truth. She performs a very important function in society although it is often a lonely role. Through the Sage, the truth is revealed, and we can see what is really there. If there is a problem, the Sage is often the one who sees and describes it. Then the Healer takes over and brings about the necessary changes or healing. In fairy tales, a wise old man or woman in the forest often discloses a secret which the hero has taken a long time to find: the waters of happiness or the meaning of life.

When we look at our lives, we find that certain people have acted as our teachers, our sages. We went to them as to a fountain, the source of knowledge and wisdom. They didn't involve themselves in our lives particularly. They were there when we sought them.

When we begin our search for the truth, we move into stage one. Our search may take us in many directions, but we are guided by our goal. We may be trying to find the right way to do things, so we turn to experts and rely on their knowledge. It may be a medical problem, for instance: we visit a doctor. We may be trying to understand our child's learning difficulty: we make an appointment with a learning specialist. We are searching for a spiritual point of view: we visit churches and read books. Sometimes we face the dilemma that different experts give us different advice. What do we do?

When my daughter was diagnosed as having scoliosis, a curvature of the spine, we consulted four different orthopedic surgeons. Each gave us a different way to treat the problem. We became very confused. No one said that there was only one right way. We found ourselves having to make a difficult choice. When we are researching the solution to a dilemma, we are at stage one of the Sage archetype. After listening to the advice of experts, we have to rely on our own inner wisdom or intuition to make the decision. We have to trust the Inner Sage.

When I was a young teacher in a fledgling school, I looked forward to having visiting experts observe our classes and attend our faculty meetings to give advice and answer our questions. One time, two experts came at the same time. In response to a question, each gave a different reply. I looked from one to the other and back again.

Was this really so? What was I to believe? I then realized that there was no single right answer. I would have to consider their advice and come to my own decision. I felt a tremendous sense of freedom. This experience is typical of the second stage of being a Sage. At stage two we doubt, question, weigh the evidence, play the devil's advocate, test all opinions against our own experience. We recognize that there is no one truth that applies to all circumstances.

We enter stage three when we realize that we must live within contradictions. We learn that we must make choices even if we can never know the exact truth.

We all have the Sage within. We have a sense for what is right. We know on a deep level that certain things are so, and others are not. I once asked my teacher how I would know if something was true. He replied that he had three ways of determining whether to accept a statement as true. First, he said, were those things which his own experience told him were true and so he didn't question them. Second were those things which he thought could be true and so he accepted these as working hypotheses with the caveat, 'Maybe'. Third were things which he could not even presume to judge because they were so far from his experience. 'I won't take these on faith, but I won't declare them as true either. I'll let them be unless at some time I have an experience that changes my position.' His process allowed for doubt and questioning while helping him remain open-minded.

Rudolf Steiner is an example of a Sage who welcomes questioning. He said, 'I beg of you now … never to accept on authority or on faith anything I have said or shall say … It is far from my intention … to lay down dogmas and claim that the facts are such and such and must be believed.'[7]

The negative aspect of the Sage is seen in the person who is convinced that she knows the truth and allows no questions or doubts. 'My truth is the truth. Accept it. If you don't, you are in peril.' This attitude allows no freedom. It strangles our minds. We may question whether we can call such a person a Sage. Although some will look up to her as a giver of wisdom, it does not seem that this approach is appropriate for our time of individuality and freedom.

12. The Fool

In Shakespeare's plays, fools play an important role. Only a fool can get away with disagreeing with the king, albeit in a joking manner. The Fool often says something much wiser than the king, while the king may truly be foolish. The king becomes the fool and the fool the king. The Fool gets away with speaking her wisdom only because everyone knows that she is a fool. She can mention a forbidden subject, which no one else dares to mention. Once it's been mentioned, the unspeakable must be acknowledged and dealt with even though it was the Fool who said it. This is the value of the Fool.

How often someone goes to the heart of the matter and then says, 'I was just joking'. To admit that the comment was serious would risk confronting those who wield power in the group. In this way, we can laugh at the fool even though the truth hurts. We accept the truth from the Fool because it seems not to threaten us.

The Fool, also known as the Trickster, appears in myths through-out the world. The Trickster is playful, full of life, childlike, willing to try anything. The Fool is willing to risk because she isn't loaded down with responsibilities. Spontaneity, silliness, and fun are elements of the Fool.

The stage one Fool enjoys life, doesn't take things too seriously, laughs at difficulties. The Fool plays.

At stage two, however, the Fool becomes the Trickster, the Clever Fool. The Fool tells the truth but in ways that will not offend. The Fool uses intelligence, puns, playing on words to shed light on a problem.

At stage three, the Fool becomes the Wise Fool. The joy of living is at the center of the Fool's life. She enjoys each moment of life, lives freely, and values the present.

In Russian tradition, holy fools were revered as 'men of God' for their ascetic ways and prophetic utterances. They had a place in the courts of Muscovy, acting as a combination of father confessor and royal soothsayer. Like Old Testament prophets, they prophesied the end of the world, called for purification, and an end to decadent ways. They often traveled widely and knew the ways of the world.

The Fool carries much of the sanguine temperament and the Social Innovator soul gesture. Mercurial, whimsical, and ever-changing, the Fool lives as a will-o'-the-wisp or an Innocent on the outside while carrying aspects of the Sage within.

The negative side of the Fool is seen when she uses humor as a weapon against others, such as the sarcastic put-down that cuts to the core. Fools also may use their insight to manipulate those around them. They may use foolishness to mask their cleverness for bad purposes. Their play-acting can become so serious that foolishness becomes madness. Playing the fool, Hamlet ends up destroying Ophelia.

Chapter 2. The Archetypes as Stages of the Human Journey

The twelve archetypes can relate to three distinct stages of life: **Preparation for the Journey, The Journey,** and **The Return from the Journey.** These are similar to the three stages described in the transformation of the temperaments in an earlier chapter. The three stages represent a maturing process. I have drawn on the work of Carol Pearson, author of *Awakening the Heroes Within: Twelve Archetypes to Help Us Find Ourselves and Transform Our World,*[1] and Joseph Campbell's *The Hero with a Thousand Faces,*[2] which I have expanded out of my own experiences and understanding.

Preparing for the journey

1. We begin our journey in the protective arms of our parents. If they have surrounded us with love and care, we experience the world as good and our place in it as secure. We are **Innocents.**

2. Some of us have had unfortunate experiences in early childhood. Out of neglect or abuse, traumatic experience or indifference, some of us come to feel that we are **Orphans.** Because we then feel that the world is not all good, we feel disappointed, betrayed, and abandoned. Everyone will go through a stage of feeling that he is alone. What we learn in this stage is that we cannot rely on others to take care of us, that we must start taking care of ourselves. When we experience ourselves as Orphans, we feel alone and helpless, and we reach out for companionship.

3. We must learn to set goals and figure out how to achieve them. This planning stage is characteristic of the **Warrior** archetype. We see the world as an arena in which to conquer and overcome. We develop discipline and courage to strike out in pursuit of our goals.

4. Then, as **Caretakers,** we realize that we cannot be aware of only our own outer goals and intentions, but we must also take care of other people's needs. This archetype awakens the social impulse in our lives.

With these capacities of innocence, independence, discipline, courage, and nurturing, we set off on our journey. Our eyes are focused on a distant horizon.

The Journey

5. As we proceed on our journey, we may experience a barrenness and loneliness of life because we are not satisfied with who we are. We seek something that is beyond us, something greater. As **Seekers,** we long for something that will bring a sense of fulfilment, and we strive to satisfy that longing, regardless of cost.

6. Along the way, we meet death. As **Destroyers,** we learn that we must give up what we have been and become someone new. This step often involves suffering as we destroy the past by letting it die.

7. Once we have let go, we can relate to life in a new way. As **Lover,** we awaken love and commitment in our hearts. We reach out to other people. Although we learn important lessons from this, we also find that commitment to others initially limits our freedom. Then we learn that a higher level of freedom exists which we have not yet achieved. Through being the Lover, we learn lessons from life. Part of loving is embracing several aspects of ourselves and others, especially the opposite or complementary aspect. In integrating masculine and feminine qualities, the Lover gives birth to something new.

8. As **Creators,** we learn to express ourselves and be creative in a new way. For example, we find undeveloped areas of ourselves, areas we may have neglected, and we start to pay attention to them. Once we have found the ability to be creative and work on our own development, we are prepared to return to the community which we left when we began our journey.

Once we have learned the lessons of our journey and have become clear about our striving, have learned to let go of the past, have awakened love and commitment, and have learned to be creative, expressive human beings, we have enhanced our souls. Our inner life is balanced with the outer, and we are clearer about who we are and what we aim for in life. We feel the power and strength of having come through life's barrenness and loneliness to a new beginning. Now we must take hold of these qualities in order to bring perspective to them. What we have learned we must now share with our community in The Return.

The Return

9. We come to realize we are the **Rulers** of ourselves and we must take responsibility for ourselves with our newly-won capacities. From this realization is born a new sense of confidence and clarity.

10. In addition to being rulers of ourselves, we find that new capacities are awakening so that we become **Healers** or Transformers of ourselves. That which has been must now become something else. Rather than seeking single answers to questions, we look at life in a new way. Rather than asking, 'What is the answer to my question?' we ask, 'How can I ask the question differently so that several possibilities arise?' 'What is the healing response so that the real nature of the dilemma is resolved?' Instead of the quick and obvious solutions, we look for solutions that will help people grow.

11. Now we must step back and reflect on the transformation we have experienced. From this vantage point as **Sages,** we can develop wisdom and perspective, objectivity and devotion to truth. This is a great gift we can offer to our communities. We may accomplish this only in special, shining moments, but it is to be celebrated nevertheless.

12. As **Fools,** we learn to live in the moment, risking security for spontaneity, and experiencing joy. We can transform the Silly Fool into the Wise Fool who combines wisdom with joy, and quiet reflection with spontaneity.

Every time we have a new experience, we participate in the journey of archetypes.

PREPARE FOR THE JOURNEY
Innocent
Orphan
Warrior
Caretaker
EXPERIENCE THE JOURNEY
Seeker
Destroyer
Lover
Creator
RETURN FROM THE JOURNEY
Ruler
Healer
Sage
Fool

Then we begin a new journey, starting once again with Innocent, Orphan, Warrior, and Caretaker.

In general, we can liken these three stages of Preparation, Journey, and Return to the three broad periods of life: from birth to age 21, age 21 to 42, and 42 onwards.

In the first stage, **Preparation for the Journey,** we, as **Innocents, Orphans, Warriors,** and **Caretakers,** explore our relation to our families, teachers, friends, and to the world. We learn to present ourselves, deal with early disappointments, define goals, and begin to care about other people as well as ourselves.

In the second stage, **The Journey,** as **Seeker, Destroyer, Lover,** and **Creator,** we have many experiences in which we find that outer things no longer satisfy us. As we confront loneliness and the dying of old ways, we have to let go of earlier habits and goals, and so we turn our search inward to seek fulfillment. Gradually a new power awakens. Out of this may emerge a new love for the world and acceptance of our destiny. We have new energies with which to express ourselves and find creative solutions to life.

In the third stage, **The Return from the Journey,** from age 42 on, we experience a maturing, a ripening of our capacities. We become **Rulers** of our desires, passions, and appetites; **Healers** of ourselves, healing the wounds from earlier years; developing perspective and objectivity as **Sages;** and then learning as the **Fool** to live in the moment, accepting the joys and sweetness of life without expectations.

We tend to think of the hero as the warrior, charging into battle, fighting for the right and conquering the wrong. But there are different ways of being heroic. The healer, the wise person, the person who brings change, the responsible committed person – each has heroic qualities. Expanding our definition of hero, from warrior to healer and wise person, encompasses a wider range of personalities, freeing us from the stereotype of the knight in shining armor, or at least extending this image to other forms of heroism.

Understanding the concept of hero or heroine as multifaceted and many-dimensional is especially important when considering feminine archetypes, because the broader definition of hero also honors the various aspects of feminine nature as valuable and heroic. It allows women to find their unique representation instead of attempting to become 'men in women's clothing'. In addition, it allows men the possibility of expressing heroism in ways different from the warrior image so strongly emphasized in western culture.

Through a broader understanding of the archetypes, we find images for those trying to solve problems through a new way of thinking, through conflict resolution, and through peaceful means rather than through military force. The concept of Peacemaker as a male image opens up many possibilities for seeing the strong, powerful male in a new way.

While each archetype, in its transformed stage, shows the best in us, in its early stages it is a hindrance, limiting and confining our self-definition. As we mature, we recognize and accept the archetype as a necessary part of our journey. The archetypes appear, present themselves to be reckoned with, disappear from view, hide, dominate, confront, challenge, and beckon us to penetrate their depths.

Synthesizing opposite archetypes on the journey towards wholeness

The archetypes often appear in pairs; and at first it seems that one is opposing the other. Yet when we synthesize the opposites, the journeying pilgrim can reach a new level of equilibrium and wholeness.

1. Innocent and Orphan – finding security in the world

Both characterize aspects of childhood; the Innocent develops trust and optimism, the Orphan develops a sense of betrayal and disappointment. The extreme Innocent is naive and unaware of the dangers in the world. The extreme Orphan, a victim of pain and suffering, distrusts people and becomes cynical. Our childhood experiences influence whether we view the world more from the Innocent's or the Orphan's perspective. Are we able to trust the world, or do we fear it and build around ourselves armor for protection? Do we feel secure or are we always looking for someone to bring us security? Do we trust or do we expect betrayal? Understanding and balancing the two archetypes enables us to walk the line between trust and vulnerability. We learn when to risk ourselves with other people and when to be wary and protect ourselves.

2. Seeker and Lover – seeking our identity

Both archetypes have to do with finding one's identity. As Seekers, we look for our identities by leaving home, by exploring paths untrod, by discovering how we differ from others. As we wander the world, we meet many trials along the way. We learn to cope with loneliness and self-doubt. We brave the wilds and the winds, searching for an understanding of our particular destiny.

As Lovers, we also look for our identities. Rather than finding them by going out into the world, however, we take the path to the soul. By loving others, we find ourselves. Rather than seeking to differentiate, Lovers seek to unite.

It may seem at first that the two paths point in opposite directions. If we take the inner path to finding our identity, it seems that we shall have to forego the outer. If we set out on the outer path, it may distract us from the inner. At different times of our lives, one path or the other will satisfy our longing. At a certain point, we come to understand that there is no contradiction, that each is an aspect of the other, as yin and yang are parts of a whole. In resolving the two paths, we find our real identity. The inner is the outer, the outer is the inner. Together they are one.

3. Warrior and Caregiver – assuming responsibility in the world

As Warriors, we identify problems as something to be conquered. We appoint ourselves to solve problems and save the victims. As Caregivers, we are less interested in conquering than in nurturing. Either archetype can take us too far in one direction. We can focus on the goal and step on people along the way, or we can become so involved in soothing someone's hurts that we do not address underlying problems. To achieve balanced action, we need to appreciate the process, to allow new things to happen without losing sight of the goal. This dilemma confronts every leader – how far do I go in one direction or the other?

4. Destroyer and Creator – establishing the true self

As Destroyer, we break down old facades, the false masks we present to the world. We experience loss without yet being mature enough to understand what is being gained. When the Destroyer is too strong, a person may feel depressed and empty. As Creator, we reconstruct our selves. Acting out of truth and clarity, we build up the authentic center of ourselves. Personal growth is an expression of the Creator at work. When the Destroyer dominates, we experience only the tragedy of life. Hanging on to the old view of what we once were, we cannot go forward. We are lost in the past. When the Creator dominates, we frantically seek out one experience after another, trying on new aspects of the self without integrating them. Only a dynamic balance of the two brings a true possibility of finding the authentic self.

5. Healer and Ruler – what is my relation to power?

Both the Healer and the Ruler express themselves through the use of power. The Healer uses power to awaken new possibilities in the other person. Tranforming one thing into another, understanding secrets living beneath the surface, the Healer uses power for the benefit of the other, whereas the Ruler uses power to establish boundaries, rules, ways of living. The Ruler justifies the use of power to bring order to society or to inner life. If the Healer is too one-sided, he uses his understanding of human nature to exploit or manipulate people. The one-sided Ruler – the tyrant – uses power over others as a way of establishing only outer order. The Healer can err on the side of too much movement, so that a center is lacking. The Ruler can err on the side of too much rigidity, so that there is no breathing room or freedom. A sensitive balance of the two is seen in the thoughtful and compassionate ruler who establishes sensible boundaries while taking people's needs into account. This balance is expressed in the concept of administration as 'servant leadership', a term applied to a new style of administration.

6. The Sage and the Fool – how do I find freedom?

The Sage needs to have the big picture, to see what is happening on the grand scale without being worried by the details. Wisdom is gained through understanding this and being able to communicate it to others. When we act as Sages and understand the broad picture, we experience freedom. This means that we grasp why our lives unfold the way they do, how human consciousness develops, how human communities evolve, what the moving forces in history are. This then leaves us free to recognize our own unique contributions.

The Fool does not step back to gain the big picture, but enters directly into life, living in the present, and enjoying the moment. The Fool experiences freedom, unbound by tradition or convention, by refusing to be labeled or restricted. As Fools we feel free because we are willing to adjust our relationship to others and to the community depending on circumstances, to continually see things through fresh eyes. Thus, the Fool in his freedom can step into any situation, look at it in a fresh way, bring humor and joviality, and not be worried about what others think.

We need to feel both sides of freedom: the side which comes through understanding; and the side which comes through spontaneity, through acting without being hindered by tradition or other people's expectations.

SECTION IV

SELF-DEVELOPMENT: STRIVING FOR WHOLENESS

Chapter 1. Facing Change, Making Change

Change transforms our lives. There are two types of changes, those we initiate and those which are involuntary. Some changes blow into our lives like cold winter gales – expected but still unpleasant. Although we can anticipate changes and can prepare ourselves for them, we can never know how they will turn out. Yet change is a necessary element of life, prompting us to discard old rigid patterns and undergo transformation. Such change can be an artistic process, in which we are the artists. If someone else *tells* us to change, though, we may feel resentment and hurt. The best change comes about because we recognize the need to do so.

I. Change which happens to us

The first kind of change is that which comes to us seemingly 'out of the blue', and after which our lives are never the same again. These include major illnesses, deaths, loss of job, unexpected pregnancy. Some major changes happen to us because we happen to live where natural disasters such as earthquakes, hurricanes and tornadoes occur. Changes also come through accidents in trains, planes, cars, and bicycles, from cataclysms such as war, and from crimes committed against us. These changes may result in the loss of our home, our job, our community; or they may simply leave us with a diminished sense of trust and security, knowing they can recur. How do we respond to these changes, so that rather than being weakened or destroyed, we continue to grow?

Two significant changes that happen to us come about through the end of a relationship and through growing older.

Losses such as the end of a relationship are often death-experiences: we can pass through the same seven stages of grief which Dr. Elisabeth Kübler-Ross describes in connection with the death of a loved one.[1] These are: *disbelief, denial, making bargains, anger, despair and depression, resignation and acceptance,* and *moving on.* The discovery that a partner is having an affair, the announcement that he or she is leaving the relationship, or the awareness of both partners that the relationship has come to an end – are all similar to death experiences.

1. Disbelief. This isn't happening. That's not really what the letter (phone call, conversation) meant. I must have misunderstood. I feel numb.

2. Denial. This is not happening to me. Other people deal with this. I've had a good marriage. We've been so close. He (or she) is upset and will look at things differently in a while. It was just a little flirtation. It won't amount to anything. I'll just be very supportive and nice. I'll take special pains with the way I look. We won't argue. You'll see. It'll be ok.

3. Bargaining. Bargaining is an attempt to deny the irreversibility of the change. Here, facing the end of a relationship is different from loss through death. In the former case, there still are opportunities for further growth and relationship during life, even if it is in another form. The possibility of reconciliation exists, at least theoretically.

'If we go to counseling or to see our priest, (minister, rabbi) then I'll accept what decision you come to.'

'If we can wait until the children are older... '

'If you continue to support me while I finish my education, then... '

'If we can keep it private for a while... '

'If I can get used to the idea first... '

'If we can remain friends... '

The strongest bargaining point is usually, 'I'll change, so you'll love me again. I'll do whatever it takes.'

The other person may agree to some part of the bargain. This creates time for rethinking, time for impulsive feelings to settle down, for going to counseling, recognizing the problems, wanting to do something about them. All of these situations allow time for rethinking and for new possibilities.

4. Anger. The feelings become more intense. 'Why are you doing this? You are wrecking years of the work that we've put into this relationship? How can you just walk out? Am I not good enough for you? Is that it? You want someone younger (prettier, more hand-some)? You aren't so great either. I'll tell everyone about you, you miserable wretch!'

During this stage, we react furiously, erratically, even violently. 'If I can't have you, no one else will!' We can't control our anger and look for ways of getting revenge. We may be blinded by our rage and act irrationally. It is at this stage of loss that violent acts are often committed.

5. Despair and Depression. Nothing has worked. The relationship is over. One feels totally helpless. During this stage some people become dependent on pills or alcohol to get through. We may withdraw, go into isolation, not answer the telephone or doorbell. We lose contact with others and may harm ourselves.

The day-in, day-out support of a few trusted friends is essential. If our regular routine can be followed – eating, sleeping, going to work – then we can mark time until an inner healing occurs. Time is the greatest healer. During this stage, we should not make any major life decisions because we are especially vulnerable to other people's advice.

6. Resignation and Acceptance. After a while (weeks, months, years), the feelings of helplessness and self-pity can give way to acceptance. Once we realize that there is no way out, something new begins to happen. One day we wake up and feel we are on the other side of a chasm. The sunrise is beautiful. The new day is lovely, and for the first time in a long time we look forward to what the day will bring. We have dropped out of life for a time, but now it's time to rejoin the human community. Gradually we begin to see friends again, go out for an evening, accept dinner invitations. There is nothing we can do to reverse the original heartbreak, so we make the best of it.

7. Moving on. Once we have resolved to move on, it is time to re-evaluate and rebuild. We have an increased ability to make decisions.

It seems that we are drawing renewed strength from somewhere beyond ourselves. We assess what we have learned, whether anything positive has come from it. We become capable of forgiveness. We let go.

Growing Older

All of us face growing older, which is also an encounter with death. Here too we go through these stages to reach acceptance.

1. Disbelief. 'I'm not old! Getting older is something that happens to other people. It won't happen to me. How come I can't do the kinds of things I used to do unless I work harder? My legs are stiff, my back aches.'

2. Despair and Denial. 'It's not age. I just sprained my muscle, that's all. My hair isn't turning grey, it's just an odd quirk. It'll slow down. I had an aunt who was gray at 30, and she's young and spry. The boss is demanding more. It's not that I can't keep up.'

3. Bargaining. 'I'll get more sleep and pay more attention to my diet, so I'll stay young. I'll hang around younger people. I'll dress younger. I'll act younger. I'll join a mountain-climbing group. I look quite dashing driving that little red sports car. If I dye my hair, use skin creams, wear a toupee, I'll still be attractive. If I can become head of my department, then I'll accept getting older and retire. If you let me play my favorite role in *Macbeth* – I've been wanting to do this throughout my career – then I'll be satisfied. Let me just earn a million before I get too old to enjoy it.'

4. Anger. 'Why aren't all the things I've done to stay young working? I've wasted so much time and energy. I thought it would never happen to me.'

5. Despair and Depression. 'It's not working. Those are wrinkles in my face. I feel more aches and pains. People refer to me as *Sir, Madame, Mister, Mrs.* They hold the door for me, ask if I need help carrying a package. I haven't accomplished so much of what I wanted to in my life. What has it all been for? I don't want to be an old man or old woman, walking slowly along the street leaning on a cane. I don't want to retire. There's nothing to do. I feel so lonely!'

5. Resignation and Acceptance. 'There's no denying it – We all get older! I may as well make the most of it. I'll have more time to devote to hobbies. I've always wanted to start a garden on the south side of the house. At least I have some friends in the same situation. I have so many memories of my life! It has been fulfilling. Even if I get too old to get around, I will feel that I've had a wonderful, blessed life.'

6. Moving On. 'I have such a different sense of appreciation. Thank you, God, for this beautiful world. Thank you, family and friends, for your love and support. Let me see how I can do things for others now. Where am I needed?'

Some move quickly through these stages; others take years. Some become stuck at one stage for a long time. Friendship is one of the strongest aids in moving through these periods. We need to describe the feelings we are experiencing. They are valid feelings for the moment. But wallowing too long in guilt or anger drains our life forces and keeps us from doing our real tasks. Friends can give us a little push now and then, but we usually have to go through each stage until we are ready to move on.

II. Changes which we choose to make

Many of the changes that we go through in life are barely noticed by others. These are the changes which we ourselves initiate, where an individual quietly and privately tries to transform his temperament, soul attitude, or viewpoint, tries to strengthen observation, overcome weaknesses, face fears, become more objective, or develop courage.

We set out to make these changes when we feel that we are no longer functioning healthily. There are times when we know that we must change, but we don't want to. We fear change, we fear what is new and unknown, even though we may be excited by it.

When we make New Year's resolutions, we are acknowledging the need to change. Every time we try to break a habit, we are trying to change. There is the old quip, 'It's easy to quit smoking – I've done it a dozen times', which acknowledges the stubbornness of habits and the difficulty of breaking them. Becoming realistic about how much change to aim for is part of what we learn.

Trying to change ourselves involves decisions. It is helpful if they are not rash decisions, which often look very different the next day. It is advisable to give ourselves three nights before making a big decision. Immediately before going to sleep we can ask the question we are trying to resolve, offer it up so to speak. In the morning, we need to listen very quietly to what comes to us. Those moments just before full waking are special times to take in new thoughts and to examine them in the light of morning. Meditation and prayer are very strong sources of help when we are making major decisions.

A thoughtful approach to decision-making has been developed by Dr. Ira Progoff, who suggests that we set up a notebook divided into different sections, and write in each of these sections.

For example, one section is called, 'Conversation with My Body'. Others are: 'Conversation with My Work', 'Conversation with My Children', 'Conversation with My Spouse'. (Others include friends, house, etc.) Clearing one's thoughts and sitting down quietly, writing a letter to this aspect of oneself or one's environment can bring to consciousness thoughts that have been hovering about but without clarity and focus. One evening, after two hours of writing a letter, 'Conversation with My Work', I found that I had a clear picture of changes I needed to make in my job. Until then, I had had difficulty focusing on the issues.

We are responsible for the decisions we make. Doing something only because someone else has told us to do it weakens our ego development. It is helpful to get advice from other people, but at some point we should stop seeking advice, make the decision in the privacy of our own hearts, and then live with the consequences.

Overcoming fear

One of the greatest obstacles to changes is fear. Fear is increasingly an illness in our culture. We fear location (heights, depths, closed places), blushing, animals, illness, and especially dying. In fear we feel confined and isolated. What happens when people feel intense fear? They turn pale, break into a cold sweat, the heart pounds, and they may feel that they are going to die at any minute. Fear affects the soul, even when there is no physical threat.

Some people develop a fear of going places. What if I die there? How will my death be? They can't sleep for fear of dying in their sleep. Others cannot go to work; they cannot be in the same room with many people. Such neuroses can take years to work through.

Fear is a basic human phenomenon. When we are young and live very protected lives, we do not commonly experience fear. Fear comes when something threatens from outside or when something separates us from the protective shelter of our family. However, we cannot remain protected forever. On the one hand our ego, our 'I', craves to separate itself, to gain independence; but on the other hand, our 'I' experiences isolation and separation as threatening and frightening. Conquering fear leads to freedom and individuality, while failure to overcome fear leads slowly to deepening anxiety.

Through knowledge and insight, we can identify our fears and overcome anxiety. *Identifying* what we fear is the first step to recovery. We acquire knowledge by looking at those things which threaten us, which make us feel lonely and isolated. Symptoms of fear help us realize that there are deeper problems, and also contain the key to overcoming and healing fear. When we understand the situation that provokes anxiety in us, our 'I' wakes up in order to overcome and triumph over it. Overcoming fear strengthens us.

Fear can weaken us if we become caught in it and don't break the cycle. About twenty years ago, my city was in the grip of fear because of a rapist who inflicted terrible punishment on his victims. For months, police could not catch him, and people began to put extra locks on doors and windows and take extra precautions. Vigilante groups patrolled streets. Panic ruled. I remember sleeping with lights on, even gathering my children into one room and sleeping with them.

Then one evening, driving home from a school excursion to San Francisco, I crossed the bridge leading to Sacramento and glanced at the twinkling lights of thousands of homes.

'What makes you think that out of all the houses in this city, the rapist will choose yours? Stop focusing so much on this,' I told myself. For the first time in months, I was able to laugh at the situation, still taking the necessary precautions, but not allowing fear to rule my life.

Today we live with constant fear because many world events are legitimately frightening — war, violence, environmental destruction. But we must counteract such fear with hope, not allowing ourselves to be traumatized by the dangers. Following are two meditations which help to strengthen us against fear.

> *We must eradicate from the soul all fear and*
> *terror of what comes out of the future.*
> *We must acquire serenity in all feelings and*
> *sensations about the future.*
> *We must look forward with absolute equanimity*
> *to everything that may come, and*
> *we must think only that whatever comes is given*
> *to us by world direction full of wisdom.*
> *It is part of what we must learn in this age,*
> *namely to live out of pure trust...*
> *without any security in existence, trusting in the*
> *ever present help of the spiritual world.*
> *Truly nothing else will do if our courage is not to*
> *fail: let us discipline our will...*
> *And let us seek the awakening from within*
> *ourselves every morning and every evening.* [2]

And the following by Adam Bittleston:

> *May the events that seek me*
> *Come unto me;*
> *May I receive them*
> *With a quiet mind*
> *Through the father's ground of peace*
> *On which we walk.*

May the people who seek me
Come unto me.
May I receive them
With an understanding heart
Through the Christ's stream of love
In which we live.

May the spirits which seek me
Come unto me;
May I receive them
With a clear soul
Through the healing Spirit's Light
By which we see. [3]

The changes we choose to make sometimes have a strong effect on society. Out of a difficult situation we have had to face, we may gain the strength to help others. After Candy Lightner's child was killed by a drunken driver, for example, she organized MADD – Mothers Against Drunk Driving – to educate people about driving while drinking and to press for stiffer penalties on drunken drivers.

Another couple had a child born with a rare disease. Through devotion to their child and later in his memory, they formed a foundation for the cure of that disease. A couple whose baby had suffered damage at birth set out to learn about residential care for severely damaged children. When they visited many homes for such children, they didn't like what they saw, and they changed their lives significantly, becoming professionals in this field and opening their own care home for children with such needs. Thus they improved the lives of many other children besides their own.

Many people mourning the passing of friends from AIDS have worked to call attention to this disease and to increase society's understanding of it.

Some people make changes that have a sweeping effect. They make the change because they grasp the significance of the challenge and are capable of doing something about it.

Biologist Rachel Carson studied the effects of pesticides, and wrote the book *Silent Spring,* which challenged the big chemical companies. President Kennedy read the book and was influenced by it.

Dr. Helen Caldecott founded *Physicians for Social Responsibility,* an organization of 23,000 doctors from many countries, who educated their colleagues about the health consequences of nuclear war, nuclear power, and nuclear weapons. Her work provided a forum for doctors from mutually hostile countries, such as the Soviet Union and the United States, to speak about those issues from the standpoint of human health rather than from a political perspective. Their common work helped end many illusions about the survivability of nuclear war and very directly influenced both Soviet and US leaders.

Barbara Wiedner had been busy raising her large family in Sacramento, California, when she was invited by a friend to attend a demonstration against nuclear arms outside the gates of a nearby Air Force base. Impulsively, she joined the demonstration and was arrested. Embarrassed, she phoned her son to get her from jail.

Her five-year-old grandson answered the phone.

'Grandma,' he said, 'I saw you on the evening news! You are going to save the world!'

This was the inspiration for her to found Grandmothers for Peace which has become a world movement of grandparents striving to bring about a safer, better world for everyone's grandchildren. Barbara Wiedner's new commitment made her an emissary to world leaders on behalf of the world's grandchildren.

In our own lives we also have the possibility of instigating change. To do this, we must imagine what is possible. This imagination can carry us through all the difficult times ahead. It provides us with an image of a world waiting to be healed. A person with this kind of imagination usually has a strong belief in a higher power. We can feel the support of other people and the blessings of the spiritual world. With such support anything is possible.

When we make changes, we face choices all along the way. How we make choices is often a reflection of our personal values and view of life. As we become more confidently aware of our own higher selves, our 'I', our choices become clearer, even if they don't become easier.

Chapter 2. Paths of Transformation

In ancient times, initiation into sacred paths at secret mystery centers provided a select few with opportunities for self-development; but nowadays a modern path is open to all who wish it. One need not pass a test or withdraw into the desert, as spiritual development can be part of our active life in the modern world. We can work on our spiritual development in the way we overcome misunderstandings, the way we forgive those who have misjudged us, or by the way we renew ourselves in nature. The modern path is so rooted in freedom that nothing compels us except our own higher self. The purpose of such self-development is not to gain powers with which to control other people or events or for other egoistic reasons. Self-development is a path by which we can become more clear and conscious in our relationship to the spiritual world. Whatever capacities we gain should not be used solely for our own benefit, but to help others. Moral development goes hand-in-hand with soul development.

Three paths of transformation

Most of the preparation for spiritual development has to do with strengthening our soul forces of thinking, feeling and willing. We can do this in three main ways: study; exercises, meditation and artistic work; and social action and interaction.

I. The path of study

The first path is through study. Learning what others have said about the spiritual world focuses our attention in this area, and in time affects the quality of our own thoughts. Poetry, inspirational writings, prayers, parables, fairy tales and great myths give us images to ponder and ideas to think about which help lift our thoughts in the direction of the eternal. Reading biographies helps us see how destiny works in the lives of human beings. Reading and studying works of spiritual teachers can loosen our thoughts from our physical needs. Every religion has a path of study which can be followed, or we can read the works of many spiritual leaders, each of whom points us in a particular direction to the spiritual world, where all the paths are united.

II. The path of experience

The second way is through experiences which we ourselves gather. Meditative and concentration exercises take us further than reading about the spiritual world, creating experiences through which we gain a direct relationship with it. These experiences include various exercises which take us into the quiet places of our souls and help awaken soul forces which are otherwise asleep.

Observation of our inner life

Rhythmic exercises are those in which we regularly review our day, our week, our year. For example, every night before going to sleep, we can picture each of the activities we did during the day, starting with the last activity we did and working backward to waking up in the morning. Doing this backward brings special strength to the 'I' and helps objectify the experiences of the day. Practising this regularly brings inner structure to one's life.

Another useful exercise is to picture the people who have been important to us at different times of our life. After working with this regularly, we may begin to see how our destiny has been unfolding. Gradually we sense the spiritual direction of our life and the karma that we have been working with. Then we can become grateful even for the difficult times, so that our appreciation is quickened. As we become inwardly quieter and more reflective, we begin to see how at moments of falling asleep and waking we are especially receptive to spiritual guidance. Often we can go to sleep with a question and in the moment of waking know what we have to do.

Observation of nature

Concentration exercises – in which one focuses on one object or concept for about five minutes, pushing away all the associative thoughts which try to stream in – strengthen the will and help us focus our thinking. This activity frees the soul from dependence on the physical body. One may choose a single object to concentrate on and stay with it for a month, then choose another; or one may stay with the same object month after month.

We live in an era of sensory overload in which we are bombarded with images and information. Slogans, headlines, billboards, newspaper articles and illustrations, television and movie images, all drain our life forces and exhaust us. Many people feel exhausted by walking through a shopping mall. There is no way to absorb everything that is there. Compare this to a walk in the woods or along a beach from which we return refreshed.

Careful observation of natural phenomena allows us to enter into nature in a purposeful, objective way. As we observe a shell, a plant, or a stone each day, keeping our feelings out of our observations, we will begin to grasp the law or idea that lives in the object. As we practice this way of observing, a new way of understanding awakens. Rather than imposing ourselves on nature, nature reveals information to us about the world. We experience the opposite of sensory overload. Within our souls a sense of devotion awakens. This purifies and heals our soul lives We experience peace and serenity.

Observation exercises – such as observing the sky every morning or the moon every night, observing the same plant, or observing what someone wears – create interest in the object of our observation. Then we place today's observation next to yesterday's. After a while, we are able to see a progression over time. This not only strengthens our powers of observation, but we begin to notice change from its first stirring. For example, as we become careful observers of the sky, we can anticipate a storm. Gradually, we experience the laws behind the phenomena of the natural world. We realize how little we normally see as we rush about our lives. Such exercises increase our feelings of wonder, devotion and appreciation, and awaken new possibilities in our soul life. All these experiences strengthen the soul so that we can move into spiritual realms in a secure way, knowing that we are not going to do something we are not ready to do. It is essential to do these exercises in total freedom. They have no outward purpose, nor are we compelled to do them by outer necessity. We create the time for them and make the effort. Usually no one else is even aware that we are doing them.

Working with the seasons

Another way to develop inner capacities is to relate to life through the seasons of the year. In each season nature expresses herself differently. In summer she adorns herself in the many colors and fragrances of the flowers, the songs of birds, the flight of insects and butterflies. In the long, light-filled days, we are pulled out of ourselves, drawn to the light and attracted and distracted by the rich offerings that meet our eye.

Then summer draws to a close, the days grow shorter, the flowers drop their seeds, and nature grows quiet. As the autumn days come, it's easier to focus inwardly and to concentrate as outer darkness grows. As winter closes in on us, the days grow even shorter, climaxing in the shortest day of the year. Nature seems to sleep, although there is activity underground. We can experience the darkest time of the year as both the loneliest and the most productive for inner work: nature no longer sustains us, so we must draw all the more intensively on our own inner powers.

As days gradually grow longer and lighter, the green blades of the crocus and narcissus, harbingers of spring, burst through the earth, declaring rebirth to us. We look forward to spring breezes, to the awakening of the earth, to sowing seed in the garden. In this time of rebirth and renewal, we reach out to nature. As we participate in the cycle of the year, we can develop soul and spiritual faculties. If we consciously work with the qualities of each season, we begin to participate in the year in a new way. A larger sense of the divine enters our inner lives and ennobles them. We may learn not only about the seasons of the year but about the seasons in our soul. We find that we have times of birth, times of harvesting the fruits of our efforts, times of death, and times of taking up seeds and giving them life. In nature and in the human being similar laws are unfolding.

In ancient mystery teachings pupils witnessed the activity of the spiritual world working through all of life. In Eleusis, for example, the young Greek pupil learned about the mysteries of the seasons through the tale of Demeter and Persephone. When Hades took the young girl Persephone into the underworld, her mother Demeter mourned and nothing on the earth would flower. All was barren. Persephone henceforth had to remain in the underworld for as many months as the number of pomegranate seeds she had eaten. When she ascended to the surface of the earth again, winter turned to spring. The earth was alive in rejoicing as Demeter rejoiced to see her daughter. Yet when those months were over, Persephone had to return to the underworld. The Earth became cold and hard once more.

Thus we have a 'picture explanation' of the origin of the seasons. When this image was taken up and became active in the inner life of the pupil, he was able to experience a truth even greater than that of the seasons: that of death and resurrection.

Rachel Carson speaks of the value of such reflections:

What is the value of preserving and strengthening this sense of awe and wonder, this recognition of something beyond the boundaries of human existence? Is the exploration of the natural world just a pleasant way to pass the golden hours of childhood or is there something deeper...?

I am sure there is something much deeper, something lasting and significant. Those who dwell, as scientists or lay-men, among the beauties and mysteries of the earth are never alone or weary of life. Whatever the vexations or concerns of their personal lives, their thoughts can find paths that lead to inner contentment and to renewed excitement in living. Those who contemplate the beauty of the earth find reserves of strength that will endure as long as life lasts.[1]

The Buddha's Noble Eightfold Path

It is not so easy to strengthen our soul forces. Over and over, we may try and fail, try and fail again. One helpful path is the Buddha's Noble Eightfold Path. By cultivating our inner life in this way, we create a creative inner space from which to work outward into all aspects of our daily life. These areas of our inner life have very practical applications.

1. Right Views – Be clear about your relationship to life. What is your view of reality? Have you developed the right attitude toward this path?

2. Right Judgment – Develop your intentions. Be thoughtful when setting goals. Give full consideration to them. Separate meaningful actions from meaningless ones. Simplify. Form your judgments independently of sympathies and antipathies. Have a good reason for what you do. When convinced that you are right, stand by your decisions.

3. Right Speech – Look at your speech. How do you use speech? Is it to gossip, to fill silence, to make thoughtful conversation? What is your relationship to lying and truth telling? Do not be afraid of silence. How do you speak to other people – to your colleagues, your spouse, your parents, your children, etc.? What is the tone? What is the content? Be an accurate listener. Speak with your fellows, not too much and not too little.

4. Right Action – Weigh your actions carefully. What motivates you? Did you do something for yourself only? For others? What did you do in each circumstance? Would you do it again? Do you act to influence others against their will? Are you looking for praise for your actions? Does it matter whether anyone else knows about your deeds? When you must act out of your inner conscience, carefully weigh how you can best do this for the benefit of all concerned.

5. Right Conduct – Live in the balance between nature, job, your needs, and others' needs. Do not be too quick, nor too slow to react. Separate essential from inessential. Do not be swallowed up in life's trivialities. The Ten Commandments would be a helpful guide for this stage of the path. For example, do not murder, do not steal, do not commit adultery. Look at life as an opportunity to develop.

6. Right Effort – Set high ideals. Attempt what is realistic, but aim high. Try, but don't lose sight of your whole life. You can't transform the world overnight. Start with what you can transform – your life, your space, your job. Can you do one thing differently? Don't try everything at once.

7. Right Mindfulness – Learn what you can from life. Review your day, your week. Learn from experience. Observe other people's actions lovingly, not critically. Go over your life and remember how many people have contributed to it, how a single statement from someone who just appeared in your life for a moment, may have changed your thinking or offered you new opportunity or insight. Reviewing your life gives you a sense of the path you have chosen.

8. Right Contemplation – Every day, if possible, do exercises of contemplation and meditation. Take time, if only five minutes, to think about your life, to find what is long-lasting, and to serve it. Do exercises that strengthen your thinking, feeling, and willing.

Because the Eightfold Path strengthens soul forces and helps us become balanced human beings, it protects us from being fanatical as we proceed with self-development. These exercises are helpful even if we never pursue further exercises or meditation. They help us become more focused, more balanced human beings, better able to do our work in the world.

Another way to pursue such development and training of our soul forces is to do the six monthly exercises given by Rudolf Steiner.[2] Elsewhere these have been called the 'Six Supplementary Exercises' or the 'Six Protective Exercises'. They can be used as monthly exercises, concentrating on one each for a month and then going on to the next, or they can be used on a weekly or daily basis. There are similarities with some of the steps of the Eightfold Path.

The six basic exercises given by Rudolf Steiner
1. Guidance of the direction of thought
Develop a time of rest during which you withdraw into yourself and completely clear your mind. Concentrate fully on an image or a thought which has nothing to do with your daily duties. For example, imagine an equilateral triangle. Then dissolve it, let it go.

Then rebuild it in your mind. Then dissolve it again. Keep out all the associative thoughts that come in and out of your mind. It is important to do this daily, even if for a few minutes. It is the first step to becoming master of one's thoughts. An image of a tree, a human being, or an inanimate object such as a button or a pencil can also be used. Sentences, phrases, or even a single word can also be used for this exercise.

2. Controlling impulses of will
Most of our actions serve a purpose. This exercise depends on choosing something that is useless. Since it serves no purpose, it is a *completely free* act. Choose some action that is not necessary and do it every day at the same time. For example, you may choose to stand on a chair every day at four o'clock. Later, add a second action, and keep the first exercise going. This exercise strengthens the will.

3. Equanimity in joy and sorrow
Sympathize with joy and sorrow without so losing self-control that you give yourself over to either one. Do not fall into extremes. This creates inner calm and strengthens the feeling life. This exercise has to do with training the feelings.

4. Positivity in judgment of the world
Develop a positive attitude. See the good, the praiseworthy, the beautiful in all experiences, in all living things. Refrain from criticism. This develops appreciation for life.

5. Cultivate openness to all things
Learn on every occasion something new from everything and everybody. This keeps one flexible and awake.

6. Repeat again and again all five exercises, systematically, and in regular rotation.

These exercises strengthen us and help us develop steadiness and balance as a preparation for meditation.

Artistic activity

Artistic work is another kind of experience which strengthens us spiritually. When we immerse ourselves in artistic activity, we are refreshed and renewed as if we had just awakened from a good night's sleep. Each form of art – painting, drawing, performing or listening to music, sculpting, dance, eurythmy, poetry – puts us into touch with the creative forces of the spiritual world and enlivens the soul. We may find we crave music or painting or poetry at different times of our lives. Art therapy or art as a hobby is recognized more and more today for its power to bring harmony into our lives.

When we engage in artistic activity we often find that experiences from other aspects of our lives rise up in our consciousness. For example, we may be struggling with an idea we have been studying. Then, as we paint, or write poetry, we suddenly have an 'Aha' experience, grasping more intuitively what our heads were wrestling with. At first, the thought is seemingly unrelated, but then we see that the particular color or image is actually the thought transformed.

In artistic activity we are in touch with the unknown, the unseen, the unnamed. Allowing art to reveal things to us in the moment of inspiration takes us out of our everyday selves and lifts us onto another plane. In this sense, the product we create is less important than the process itself. As we bring more and more consciousness to the process, we sense when to impose ourselves, when to stand back, when to let go. We enter into dialogue with the Muses. Thus art becomes a path to spiritual development.

III. The Social Path

The third way is through our actions and interactions. Here we learn to work together with others to accomplish important deeds. Together we serve something bigger than ourselves. We also may work alone, but when we work with others there is the added experience of each other person's contributions to the whole. The result is something greater than any of us alone could do. Such individuals as Albert Schweitzer, Mother Theresa and Martin Luther King dedicated their lives to service and inspired the world with their example. Thousands of others, however – possibly millions – also follow this path of service, unknown to the wider world.

The path of service is, in a sense, the opposite of the path of meditation. When we do meditative work, we use our thinking powers over time and with much effort, to enhance powers of imagination, then inspiration, and finally intuition. The social path, however, begins with action based on immediate intuition of what needs to be done. Then, *after we have acted,* we gain inspiration by reflecting in quiet on what we have done. We observe the consequences of our actions. What has been the result? Finally, this leads to imagination. We gain a picture of the deed and our actions. Through this picture we learn from our actions.

This path enables us to 'do the good'. We join with others, with whom we may not necessarily feel a strong sympathetic connection, because a common vision unites us, enabling us to overcome personal difficulties in order to serve the shared task.

For those who wish to live an active life, this is a suitable path.. Spiritual life and active social life become one and the same. Deeds wake us up. We learn together and through each other. We take risks. We dare to jump in and act before we are completely spiritually developed, but the times demand it, and so we learn as we go. The key element here is inner listening – the ability to find inner quiet, to reflect on our deeds rather than moving quickly from deed to deed and losing ourselves in action. Listening is the meditative aspect of the outwardly active, social path.

It is not a matter of choosing one path exclusively. Each path develops aspects of our soul and spiritual life. We may be working on all three paths at the same time. Study, exercises in soul development and artistic disciplines, and action are three complementary paths to transformation, three ways to mould and shape our lives into new vessels for the spirit.

Chapter 3. Living in Balance

We live in a time when it seems that there is nothing that science can't eventually explain or technology manipulate. Our science gives us new technologies and our new technologies give us new science, astrophysics being one spectacular example. The unfathomable *mystery* of nature has been replaced by nature's *secrets*, waiting to be discovered and exploited. As our machines become more like people, our view of the human being increasingly resembles a machine. For many people, this worldview leaves neither room nor need for any spiritual dimension. The physical, material world has it all.

At the same time, however, and in contrast, we live in a world in which the usual limits and constraints of mortal life often seem to have been abrogated. The material world will soon be replaced by a virtual world. Whether through drugs, computer electronics or escapist entertainment, we increasingly have ways to forget that we live in mortal bodies on a physically limited planet or that we have any mortal limits. Illusion and ecstasy sweetly beckon.

I see these two tendencies as the product of two forces shaping our world. The first, which draws us ever more deeply into a physical and material worldview which scoffs at anything invisible or religiously mysterious, I call 'the contracting force'. The other, which beckons us away from the concrete and physical, I call 'the expanding force'. Our energies can be diverted by these two forces in either of two directions, or both simultaneously. Each by itself is one-sided and unhealthy. But when we work consciously with them together, they can serve us well.

The contracting force moves us in the direction of rigidity and abstraction. We place highest value on numbers, on quantitative proof, without considering the broad picture. For example, educational systems yield to this temptation when they emphasize test scores at the expense of learning. We can only trust facts and objectivity; imagination leads us astray. Because important aspects of education cannot be easily measured, we make the measurable important instead.

Charles Darwin expressed this in his journal:

> But now for many years I cannot endure to read a line of
> poetry. I have tried lately to read Shakespeare, and found it
> so intolerably dull that it nauseated me. I have also almost
> lost my taste for pictures and music. I lament this curious
> loss of my higher aesthetic tastes ... My mind seems to have
> become a kind of machine for grinding out general laws, out
> of large collections of facts, but why this should have caused
> the atrophy of that part of the brain alone, on which higher
> tastes depend, I cannot conceive.

The contracting force focuses on material life only. 'There is
nothing else, and anyone who thinks otherwise is a dreamer. How is
all this spiritual stuff going to help me in the "real world"?' This
attitude encourages us to see wonder mainly in the new possibilities
of technology, in its usefulness, efficiency, and power. We can drown
in information, especially now with the help of the computer, but
what do we learn of reality? We may worship the machine, forgetting
that the human mind designed it. For some, who express almost
religious excitement and devotion to their 'toys' or 'tools' rather than
to other human beings or to their inner life, technology has taken
the place of the spiritual life. Like other addicts, computer addicts
often lose a sense of time and space and neglect their relationships
with family or colleagues, as well as their soul and spiritual life.

The mechanistic view has become part of our everyday vocab-
ulary. 'Delete information', 'Input', 'Output'. The brain is seen merely
as a computer for processing information. When I mentioned to a ten-
year-old boy that he had a very good memory, he replied, 'That's my
hard drive'.

The expanding force, on the other hand, lifts us out of ourselves so
that we live in vague, dreamy pictures and unclear thinking. 'Don't
Worry. Be happy!' This form of thinking creates a world of illusion
which we can enter through the use of drugs, alcohol, obsessive
involvement with television, film or pornography. These illusory
worlds work on our boredom with everyday life, on the pain or
suffering we feel, on our fears. They lift us out of our lives and give

us a 'high' – at least for the moment, until we come crashing down. They tell us that what is happening in our lives is not real, and that we should therefore not invest much energy in it.

The strange thing is that the more we escape into this false spiritual world, the duller we become, the more dependent we become on substances or on illusory experiences to sustain the excitement.

It is difficult to consider a television addict (the so-called 'couch potato') or a narcotics addict as someone living an exciting or meaningful life. Instead, she is temporarily escaping the pressures of everyday life. Unfortunately, the more she succeeds in escaping, the less capable she is of taking hold of her life and experiencing its true joys and accomplishments. She probably wouldn't be able to cope with real excitement if she had it! Another, less extreme, form of escape from the challenges of daily life is nostalgia. We enthusiastically remember the past, forgetting its struggles while exaggerating and intensifying the positive. Whether it's the experiences of our childhood or events from some distant time in history, romanticizing life may add to our experiences or it may distort reality, depending on how strong such a feeling is and how it affects our ability to see what is in front of us. Bathing us in pleasurable feelings, nostalgia has the power to dissolve our objectivity about the past, preventing us from consciously taking hold of our lives in the present.

The one-sided expanding force is over-enthusiastic and over-generalizing without regard to the facts.

Another aspect of the expanding force is the feeling that little on earth really matters, that only the spiritual world is real. A resistance, even resentment, grows toward the material world. A person may move from one spiritual movement to another, seeking an immediate spiritual experience, or she may rely on drugs to produce the experience. Just as the computer addict treasures her 'toys', so the 'spiritual' addict may grow overly enthusiastic about her channeler and crystals, interpreting every act as a sign determined by celestial bodies. Karma can be used as an excuse for not taking personal responsibility for one's behavior. In the maze of spiritual influences, free will is forgotten..

The contracting force, by contrast, sometimes prompts us to see the living world as if it were mechanical, governed only by lifeless, soul-less forces. This can lead us to regard the world as only a mass of facts, of meaningless phenomena. Science, with its emphasis on statistics and models, patterns and rigid forms, is highly effective at isolating and analyzing the individual elements of problems, but it can lure us away from thinking about the problem as a whole interacting system and prevent our exercising balanced judgment. Of course newer, more holistic scientific perspectives are also increasingly emerging and gaining credence, which, instead of dissecting life into its dead constituents, recognize the wonder and mystery of the universe once more.

The middle way

Each kind of temptation – those which would disconnect us from coping with the realities of mortal life, and those which would disconnect us from coping with the realities of spiritual life – encourages us to look at life from a very narrow view, saying to us, 'Feel good. Escape into another kind of reality,' or 'This is all there is, so make the most of it.' They pull us away from our real work, which is to walk the middle way, balanced between the earthly and the spiritual worlds, which are not two separate parts of our lives but a single, complex, richly dynamic approach to life. When we walk the middle way, there are no simple solutions – which can be uncomfortable. Yet we cannot avoid the tension which exists between these two opposing forces. This is an inherent part of being human and having freedom.

Through art and beauty, the expanding force lifts us beyond the merely physical. We can rejoice in the world of form and color, in composition and pattern, in the delight of our senses. We can feel linked with creative powers and be filled with excitement. The spiritual world may feel close and accessible. Yet we cannot exist in this consciousness all the time. We need to deal with the everyday needs and realities. Otherwise, as Rudolf Steiner says, 'life takes its revenge'.[1]

Computers and other machines are helpful tools of modern life. We should use them, keeping in mind their possibilities and limitations. Wise use of computers gives us access to necessary information, such as instant weather maps which help us

understand the movements of hurricanes or tornadoes and programs which keep track of disease in various regions of the earth.
The computer is a very useful tool, but when parents and teachers
become fanatical about the need for young children to use them, the
balance is lost.

As long as we have physical bodies, we are subject to the laws of
the physical world. We eat, sleep, and we need shelter. We will
experience temptations in all these and other aspects of physical life
– in eating too much or too little, in concentrating too much on
what we eat or what we wear, or in ignoring them completely. The
same goes for our homes. We can spend every spare minute and
dollar to make them into elegant castles, or we can treat them with
utilitarian indifference to everything but the essentials. These are
extremes. We can become fanatical at either end of the spectrum,
making either indulgence or asceticism into our personal religion.

The physical world is beautiful, wonderful, and majestic, an
expression of the divine world which created it. Our food, our
clothes and our homes are all expressions of how we relate to the
physical world. I don't think that we are meant to deny these worlds
any more than we are meant to idolize them. How do we find the
balance? Our challenge is to enjoy the gifts of physical life, to appreciate their beauty, and yet to remember that there is more to life.

In our soul-life we also face temptations – desire, egotism, lust,
greed, selfishness, laziness, self-righteousness, self-satisfaction, arrogance, fanaticism and the certainty that only we have the right path
to heaven. We can be carried away with enthusiasm or we can be too
cold and indifferent; too indulgent or too judgmental; too tolerant or
too intolerant. Here again, the key to healthy development is balance.

Because each of us has an 'I', we are subject to the laws of the
spirit. In our path of self-development, spiritual laws are at work,
such as laws of destiny and karma. The life of the spirit and the life
of our physical body meet in our soul-life, which is the bridge
between the two. The soul is also the battleground where temptations live and oppose one another. Goethe is describing this when
he has Faust say,

Two souls, alas, are dwelling in my breast,
And either would be severed from its brother;

The one holds fast with joyous earthly lust
Onto the world of man with organs clinging;
The other soars impassioned from the dust,
To realms of lofty forebears winging.[2]

It is in our soul-lives that we reconcile the opposites into a third possibility – something new which has not occurred before. Each of us has her way of working in the world, of meeting the challenges to her soul-life. When we expect others to work in the same way we do, we end up battling each other, judging and isolating each other. We live in a time of heightened individuality, in which we are super-conscious of our own needs and viewpoints. Our challenge is to find ways to be an individual while living in a community and serving the needs of the group. When we are successful at doing this, creative solutions emerge that benefit our communities and our own needs. An example of this process is seen in consensus work in organizations.

Three streams of activity

Part of walking the middle way is understanding that there are various different legitimate ways to carry out our work. Bernard Lievegoed, in his book, *The Battle for the Soul*,[3] speaks of three streams of spiritual activity in which the soul is active in the world.

One is the 'cognition stream' by which one strives to gain wisdom. This is the way of the 'knowers', those who focus their lives on studying and understanding the wisdom of the ages. On this path, a person uses her thinking to develop her soul. The person very carefully thinks through what is going to happen beforehand, and then does it. Knowers can be sources of advice and inspiration. Thinking back to the earlier descriptions of soul attitudes, we can see that the members of the cognition stream tend to be Reflective Preservers or Spiritual Investigators.

The second stream is the path of transformation of matter through action. Those on this path work strongly through their wills in contrast to those who work primarily through their powers of reflection, and would include such people as the sculptor transforming a formless block of stone into a magnificent sculpture, the painter who creates an image on canvas, the farmer who transforms the earth through his work, the pharmacist who prepares health-giving medicines, the doctor who treats her patient's illness. Those who work strongly in this path are involved in processes whose outcomes are not always predictable. They carry out an action, then step back and evaluate it and try to come to an understanding of what they have done. The reflective process comes at the end of the action rather than before it. These people tend to represent such soul attitudes as Social Innovator, Active Talker, or Thinker Organizer.

The third stream is concerned specifically with development of the human soul, and works through relationship. People working in this stream work with the emotional life. This is the social path, a path on which people work together. Through gentleness and love, forces are developed which strengthen the human soul. We develop our soul forces by facing difficulties, by learning to forgive, by listening to our fellows' concerns. We can progress along this path only through involvement with others. A strong aspect of this path is sacrifice. Social workers, people who work with the handicapped, and those who give counsel and therapy – all are concerned with the health of the human soul. These people are working through the third stream. They tend to have strong Dreamy Nurturer or Radiant Balancer soul attitudes.

Each of us works with all three streams, but with emphasis on one. Each stream needs the other two to be complete. I have been a teacher for over thirty-five years, so it is natural that I use the teaching profession in the following example:

–   If I am a teacher primarily of the **first path,** I approach my subject as a scholar, focusing mainly on the content of my courses, feeling responsible for my students knowing the material that they are studying. This is the knowledge stream.

–   If I am primarily a teacher on the **second path,** working through the will, I see my work with the students as an artistic process, right down to the more artistic, open-ended way I plan my lessons. I base my teaching on creative impulse, on the will stream.

- If I am following the **third stream** – the path which works through the feelings – I approach my teaching more as a counselor, focusing on the soul-life of the students, their needs, their emotional development, what is going on in their families and in their personal relationships. I choose my subject or the way I approach the subject to meet students' emotional needs.

Ideally, I will consider all three aspects in my teaching, yet the reality is that when I look around at my colleagues, I can see that we may include all three approaches, but each of us is particularly strong in one. Seeing this enables me to appreciate my colleagues for their efforts and their ways of working instead of judging them according to my own bias or my particular stream. In this way, I can recognize the temptations that work upon my soul-life and be prepared to recognize my own one-sidedness when it occurs.

As we grow more conscious of specific areas of tension and balance within ourselves, we can work on them in our daily lives. Recognizing the contracting and expanding forces, cultivating the middle way, and appreciating the three streams of spiritual activity in which the soul is active in the world, enhances the development of our 'I'. As we do all these things, life becomes more meaningful and fruitful.

Chapter 4.
The Power of Love

We can develop ourselves in many ways – through imagination, courage, and responsibility, or through connecting ourselves with nature and working with the seasons; but the greatest power for change is that of love.

Love is a major force in the transformation of life. How can we develop love? There are three capacities which we need to develop so that love becomes a way of life.

The first is the capacity to see the divine in every human being. Who is this person who stands before me? Can I see beyond his physical appearance, occupation, personality, beyond race and nationality? Can I see the integrity of the human spirit shining through each person? As Satish Kumar, editor of the magazine *Resurgence,* expressed it:

If I go as a Hindu, I meet a Muslim, a Christian or a Jew;
If I go as an Indian, I meet a Pakistani, a Chinese or an American;
If I go as a Gandhian, I meet a socialist, a capitalist or a communist;
But if I go as a human being I meet human beings everywhere.[1]

The second is the capacity to experience the suffering of others as if it were our own.

The third capacity is being able to achieve balance within our thinking, feeling and willing. Out of the balance of soul forces, love awakens within us.

– In balanced thinking, we understand and respect the other person's reasons for doing what he does.
– In balanced feeling, we develop empathy and sympathy.
– In balanced willing, we take responsibility for our actions and have the courage and will to forgive others as well as ourselves.

Love is easy to talk about and very difficult to realize. Developing capacities for love is a lifelong task. The key to this task is overcoming preoccupation with ourselves which prevents us from connecting with our fellow human beings. If we are only stuck in ourselves, we can't move forward.

Seven stages of love

There are seven stages of love which correspond to the stages of our development – warmth, affection, desire, respect, devotion, healing, and sacrifice:

1. At the first stage, we experience love through **warmth.** We perceive it as sensation. Warmth nourishes us and helps us to grow. We can almost measure people's warmth as we meet them. Does a person exude warmth or coolness? We find ourselves responding to his 'soul temperature'. We can express warmth without directing it toward a particular person. Some people are warm in the way they approach the world; others are cooler. It may or may not be connected to a particular relationship. As infants, we depend on our parents' warmth to form a sense of security.

2. As we develop relationships with our parents and others around us, we experience **affection.** This is less tangible than warmth, more subtle, more engaging. People express affection through a smile, a pat on the back, a hug, a kiss. Through these gestures they affirm the other person and communicate their awareness and support of him. Affection is the actual communication of warmth, directed toward a specific object.

3. As our soul forces awaken in adolescence, so does **desire.** We experience need, a sense that we lack something and desperately need it, whether it be a skateboard, a concert ticket, or a relationship. Unlike stages 1 and 2 in which warmth and affection come to us from without, desire springs from within the self. Out of our personal emotional life, desire reaches out to encompass, to bring what is outside into ourselves. How do we satiate our desires? We

say, 'Oh, I love that!' about a dress in a department store window or a car in the dealer's lot. What we really mean is, 'I want it'. We love it in that we want to possess it. We can do the same with other human beings. We can confuse love and desire, and when the desire is satisfied, the relationship may be finished. By itself, desire is never enough. Yet desire awakens us to what attracts us; it motivates us to action. It may lead to love. When it takes hold of us too strongly, though, it may become an obsession, consuming us and destroying our power to love.

4. When we move beyond desire to an acknowledgement and recognition of the other person, we have moved to the fourth stage of love. Here we see that the other has a mixture of strengths and weaknesses just as we do. We come to recognize the commonality, the humanity, which we share with that other person, which enables us to treat him with respect, the same respect we wish to be treated with. This leads us out of ourselves into the other human being.

5. The fifth stage takes us even further into the other, beyond recognition and respect to reverence. Our own soul forces of **devotion** are engendered as we treasure, protect, honor, and celebrate another person.

6. As we engage with the real being of another person, a new stage awakens – that of **healing,** in the sense of 'making whole'. We sense what the other person needs to become whole and complete and we look for ways to serve that need.

7. The seventh stage is that of **sacrifice,** in which we give ourselves up for the love of the other. It is the noblest act of human existence. One hopes never to be confronted with the need to sacrifice oneself, but if it does arise, one responds.

Each of us in his own life experiences elements of these seven stages. Each of the stages also has its other side, its 'double'. For example, we may think that we are acting out of an impulse of love, but really may be motivated by egotism or false generosity. Developing ourselves along the path of the seven stages of love calls us to be conscious and reflective, to be honest with ourselves and capable of self-correction. At each stage, we are called upon to forgive others who have not loved us or who knowingly or unknowingly have done us harm. Forgiveness releases creative forces which can be used to solve problems, cultivate new relationships, and overcome difficult situations. Our own ability to love cannot flower until and unless we are able to let go and forgive.

Love is the final gift of soul weaving

Love is the most powerful creative substance of our souls. When a weaver designs a pattern, threads the loom, and patiently plies the shuttle, he gives full attention to his work. So, too, when we weave our life's tapestry, we need to give attention to the patterns, to the quality of our relationships, to our goals and achievements, to our ability to accept and forgive. When the tapestry is completed and it is time to bid goodbye to life, one hopes to be able to look back and say, 'The most important thing which I learned in life was how to love'.

Appendix

Soul Types (Section I: Chapter 1)

1. I have used aspects of the names of soul types given by the following authors:

Max Stibbe: *Seven Soul Types*, Hawthorn Press, U.K., 1992, p. 25

Active types
1. Self-conscious type – Saturn
2. Dominant type – Jupiter
3. Aggressive type – Mars

Passive types
4. Romantic type – Moon
5. Mobile or agile type – Mercury
6. Aesthetic type – Venus

Ideal type
7. Radiant type – Sun

Bernard Lievegoed: *Man on the Threshold. The Challenge of Inner Development*, Hawthorn Press, U.K., 1985, p. 115

1. Saturn – investigator
2. Moon – conserver
3. Jupiter – thinker
4. Mercury – innovator
5. Mars – entrepreneur
6. Venus – carer
7. Sun – balancer

2. According to Rudolf Steiner's research the origin of these soul qualities lies in the time between a person's death and new birth. Further information can be found in Rudolf Steiner: *Life Between Death and Rebirth. The active connection between the living and the dead.* Anthroposophic Press, New York, 1968.

3. Since ancient times, the soul qualities have been linked with planets or other celestial bodies, as well as with certain metals and mythical characters. The mythical characters are listed by their Latin names, followed by the Greek.

The Active Talker is creative, purposeful, filled with strength and energy to make things happen.
Planet: Mars.
Metal: Iron.
Mythical character: Mars or Ares, god of war.

The Nurturer Dreamer is attentive to people and their feelings, brings love and beauty to life.
Planet: Venus.
Metal: Copper.
Mythical character: Venus or Aphrodite.

The Thinker Organizer puts together the big picture, makes the plan, looks at life objectively.
Planet: Jupiter.
Metal: Tin.
Mythical character: Jupiter or Zeus.

The Social Innovator keeps things moving, brings people together, heals social wounds through flexibility and humor.
Planet: Mercury.
Metal: Mercury or quicksilver.
Mythical character: Mercury or Hermes.

The Spiritual Investigator searches for truth, tries to bring spiritual considerations into everyday life, has a deep sense of responsibility.
Planet: Saturn.
Metal: Lead.
Mythical character: Saturn or Kronos.

The Reflective Preserver remembers what has happened in the past, brings the need for routine and tradition, strong intellect, forms concepts for what is going on.
Celestial body: the Moon.
Metal: Silver.
Mythical character: Luna or Selene.

The Radiant Balancer brings healing wisdom, shines out on life, evokes the best from each, radiates love and joy.
Celestial body (more accurately a star) – the Sun.
Metal: Gold.
Mythical character: Sol or Helios.

Chapter Notes

Introdution
1   See note on gender at the end of this introduction
2   Betty Staley: *Tapestries, Weaving Life's Journey,* Hawthorn Press 1997

Section I: **Chapter 1**
1   Jerome Kagan, *Galen's Prophecy, Temperament in Human Nature,* Basic Books, New York, 1994, p. 28
2   Knud Asbjorn Lund, *Understanding Our Fellow Men,* New Knowledge Books, Sussex, U.K., 1965

Section I: **Chapter 3**
1   Lund, op. cit., pp. 22-23

Section II: **Chapter 1**
1   Edna St Vincent Millay: *Collected Poems of Edna St Vincent Millay,* Harper & Row, N.Y., 1956, p13
2   See next section

Section II: **Chapter 11**
1   Albert Einstein: *The World As I See It,* The Philosophical Library, New York, 1949
2   From materials handed out at a teacher training course, Michael Hall, England, 1959-60

Section III: **Chapter 1**
1   Joseph Campbell: *The Hero with a Thousand Faces,* Bollingen Series XVII, Princeton U. Press, Princeton, N.J., 1973, 3rd editon.
2   Carol Batdorf: *Spirit Quest: The Initiation of an Indian Boy,* Hancock House, Surrey, B.C., 1990
3   Gustav Mahler: Letter to Bruno Walter. Quoted by Henry Louis de la Grange in dustjacket notes for Capitol Records album of *The Song of the Earth.*

4   Mary Catherine Bateson: *Composing a Life: Life as a Work in Progress,* Penguin, 1990
5   Quoted by Honore Willsie Morrow in *The Father of Little Women,* Little Brown & Co, Boston, 1927
6   Johannes Hemleben: *A Documentary Biography,* Henry Golden Ltd, Sussex, 1975
7   Rudolf Steiner: *The Mission of the Folk Souls,* Rudolf Steiner Press, London, 1970

Section III: **Chapter 2**
1   Carol Pearson: *Awakening the Heroes within: Twelve Archetypes to Help Us Find Ourselves and Transform the World,* Harper, San Francisco 1991. This author characterizes the archetypes as qualities of personality. She calls the archetypes by the following names: Innocent, Orphan, Warrior, Caregiver, Seeker, Destroyer, Lover, Creator, Ruler, Magician (or Healer), Sage, and Fool. I have used Pearson's work as a foundation and expanded it out of my own experiences and understanding.
2   Joseph Campbell: *The Hero with a Thousand Faces,* Princeton University Press, New Jersey, 1968

Section IV: **Chapter 1**
1   Elizabeth Kübler-Ross: *On Death and Dying, Macmillan,* New York 1970
2   Attributed to Rudolf Steiner, and translated by René Querido. (Mr Querido says he received this verse many years ago and no longer recalls from where or whom.)
3   Adam Bittleston: *Meditative Prayers for Today,* Floris Books, Edinburgh 1982

Section IV: **Chapter 2**
1   Rachel Carson: *The Sense of Wonder,* Harper & Row, New York 1956
2   I have based my description of these six exercises on information in various books by Rudolf Steiner. Details can be found in: *An Outline of Occult Science,* translated by H.B. Monge, Anthroposophical Press, N.Y., 1949

Knowledge of Higher Worlds and its Attainment, translated by George Metaxa, Anthroposophical Press, N.Y., 1975

Theosophy: An Introduction to the Spiritual Processes in Human Life and in the Cosmos, translated by Catherine Creeger, Anthroposophic Press, N.Y., 1994

See also: Florin Lowndes: *Enlivening the Chakra of the Heart,* Rudolf Steiner Press, London 1998

Section IV: **Chapter 3**

1 *Die Kernpunkte der sozialen Frage* ('Towards Social Renewal'), Rudolf Steiner Verlag, Dornach, Switzerland 1976

2 Goethe: *Faust.* 'Outside the City Gates', lines 1112-1117. W.W. Norton & Co, N.Y., 1976

3 Bernard Lievegoed, *The Battle for the Soul,* Hawthorn Press, Stroud, U.K., 1993. pp.33-43

Section IV: **Chapter 4**

1 Satish Kumar, in his autobiography: *Path without Destination,* William Morrow, New York

Bibliography

Batdorf, Carol, *Spirit Quest, The Initiation of an Indian Boy,* Hancock House, Surrey, B.C., 1990

Baumer, Franklin L. ed., *Main Currents of Western Thought,* 4th ed. Yale University Press, New Haven, 1978

Bittleston, Adam, *Meditative Prayers for Today,* Floris, Edinburgh, 1993

Carson, Rachel, *The Sense of Wonder,* Harper & Row, New York, 1956

Easton, Stewart, *Herald of a New Epoch,* Anthroposophic Press, New York, 1980

Elliot, George, McFarland, Philip, Granite, Harvey, and Peckham, Morse, ed. *Themes in World Literature,* Houghton Mifflin, Boston, 1970

Emerson, Ralph Waldo, 'Nature' in Nature, Addresses and Lectures, A.L. Burt Co.

Hiebel, Frederick, *The Gospel of Hellas, The Mission of Ancient Greece and the Advent of Christ,* Anthroposophic Press, New York, 1949

Kübler-Ross, Elisabeth, *On Death and Dying,* Macmillan, New York, 1969

Lievegoed, Bernard, *The Battle for the Soul,* Hawthorn Press, Stroud, England, 1993

Lievegoed, Bernard, *Man on the Threshold, The challenge of inner development,* Hawthorn Press, Stroud, England, 1985

Lund, Knud Asbjorn, *Understanding Our Fellow Men,* privately printed, no date is given, out of print

Moore, Robert, *The Warrior Within, Accessing the Knight in the Male Psyche,* Avon Books, New York, 1992

Morrow, Honore Willsie, *The Father of Little Women,* Little, Brown & Co., Boston, 1927

Pearson, Carol S., *Awakening the Heroes Within, Twelve archetypes to help us find ourselves and transform our world,* Harper, San Francisco, 1991

Pearson, Carol S., *The Hero Within, Six Archetypes We Live By*

Pelikan, Wilhelm, *The Secrets of Metals,* Anthroposophic Press, Spring Valley, New York, 1973

Progoff, Ira, *Depth Psychology and Modern Man,* McGraw Hill, New York, 1959

Shakespeare, William, *The complete works of,* Clark &Wright, ed., Doubleday, New York, Vol. II

Smart, Ninian, *The Religious Experience of Mankind,* Charles Scribner's, New York, 1960

Steiner, Rudolf, *Human and Cosmic Thought,* Rudolf Steiner Press, Great Britain, 1991

Steiner, Rudolf, *Occult Science;* Rudolf Steiner Pub. Co., London, 1949

Steiner, *Intuitive Thinking as a Spiritual Path,* Anthroposophical Press, New York, 1995

Stibbe, Max, *Seven Soul Types,* Hawthorn Press, Stroud, 1992

Tolstoy, Leo, *the Works of,* Walter J. Black, Inc., New York, 1928

Wieland, Friedemann, *The Journey of the Hero,* Prism, Great Britain, 1991

Other books from Hawthorn Press

All Year Round
Ann Druitt, Christine Fynes-Clinton, Marije Rowling

Brimming with seasonal stories, activities, crafts, poems and recipes, this book offers a truly inspirational guide to celebrating festivals throughout the seasons. A sequel to *The Children's Year*, this book arises from the festivals workshops run by the authors at the annual *Lifeways* conference at Emerson College.

'The words are ours, the festivals are yours.' This book encourages both adults and children to explore forgotten corners of the educational curriculum and to develop and adapt the various festivals to fit their own family traditions. The enthusiasm and colourful creativity with which this book is written is guaranteed to stimulate interest in the diverse and multiple joys of the seasons.

288pp;250 x 200mm; fully illustrated; ISBN 1 869 890 47 7

The Children's Year
Crafts and clothes for children and parents to make
Stephanie Cooper, Christine Fynes-Clinton, Marije Rowling

You needn't be an experienced craftsperson to create beautiful things! This charmingly illustrated book encourages children and adults to try all sorts of different handwork, with different projects relating to the seasons of the year.

220pp; 250 x 200mm; paperback; illustrated; ISBN 1 869 890 00 0

Between Form and Freedom

A practical Guide to the Teenage Years

Betty Staley

Betty Staley offers a wealth of insights about teenagers, providing a compassionate, intelligent and intuitive look into the minds of children and adolescents. She explores the nature of adolescence and looks at teenagers' needs in relation to family, friends, schools, love and the arts. Issues concerning stress, depression, drug and alcohol abuse and eating disorders are included.

288pp; 210 x 135mm; paperback; illustrations; ISBN 1 869 890 08 6

To a Different Drumbeat

A Practical Guide to parenting Children with Special Needs

Patricia Clarke, Holly Kofsky, Jenni Lauruol

This is a book which aims to enhance the process of caring for children who have special needs. Based on personal experience, it is about growing, about loving and about help in this specific area of parenting.

240pp; 248 x 190mm; sewn limp binding; ISBN 1 869 890 09 4

The Lady and the Unicorn

Gottfried Buttner

The author discusses the symbolism and real significance of the beautiful but enigmatic tapestries of the Paris Cluny Museum.

128pp; 297 x 210mm; hardback; colour plates; ISBN 1 869 890 52 3

Games Children Play
How Games and Sport Help Children Develop
Kim Brooking-Payne
Illustrated by Marije Rowling

Games Children Play offers an accessible guide to games with children of age 3 upwards. These games are all tried and tested, and are the basis for the author's extensive teacher training work. The book explores children's personal development and how this is expressed in movement, play, songs and games.

Each game is clearly and simply described, with diagrams or drawings, and accompanied by an explanation of why this game is helpful at a particular age. The equipment that may be needed is basic, cheap and easily available.

192pp; 297 x 210mm; paperback; illustrations; ISBN 1 869 890 78 7

More Lifeways
Sharing Parenting and Family Paths
Edited by Patti Smith and Signe Schaefer
Foreword by Gudrun Davy and Bons Voors

Fired by continuing Lifeways workshops over the last fourteen years, *More Lifeways* offers parents further space for support and encouragement. Signe Schaefer and Patti Smith invite you to a conversation about things to question, areas to explore and things to agree with.

'Our hope for *More Lifeways* is that, through the contribution of these individuals, others may be inspired to face the challenges that come toward them and find support to journey as parents, partners and human beings.'   Gudrun Davy and Bons Voors

352pp; 216 x 150mm; paperback; photos; ISBN 1 869 890 86 8

More Precious than Light
How Dialogue can Transform Relationships and Build Community

Margreet van den Brink

Introduction by Russell Evans

Profound changes are taking place as people awaken to the experience of the Christ in themselves, and in significant human encounter. As tradition fades, individual and social paths of growth emerge. These are helped by building relationships through helping conversations, through dialogue, through exploring heartfelt questions which can lead to liberating personal insights.

160pp; 216 x 138mm; paperback; ISBN 1 869 890 83 3

Naming
Caroline Sherwood

Choosing a name for your child used to be easy! For example, you could choose from the traditional names in your family, calling them after a particular relation. However, in our multi-cultural, multi-faith society there are now so many names to choose from.

Naming is special because Caroline Sherwood first directs your attention to your experience of the essential being of your incarnating child. Sensing the unique qualities and identity of your baby, you can then use this book to find a name that matches. This is the only naming book that suggests this approach, with a comprehensive dictionary relating meanings to names, as well as the usual names index.

Having found a name, you can decide on an appropriate naming ceremony or use the examples in the book to create your own.

228pp; 246 x 189mm; paperback; illustrated; ISBN 1 869 890 55 6

Published Summer 1999.

New Eyes for Plants
A Workbook for Observing and Drawing Plants

Margaret Colquhoun and Axel Ewald

Here are fresh ways of seeing and understanding nature with a vivid journey through the seasons. Detailed facts are interwoven with artistic insights, showing how science can be practiced as an art, and how art can help science through using the holistic approach of Goethe.

Readers are helped by simple observation exercises, by inspiring illustrations which make a companion guide to plant growth around the year. A wide variety of common plants are beautifully drawn, from seed and bud to flower and fruit.

Dr Margaret Colquhoun researches into plants and landscape. Axel Ewald is a sculptor. The book is the outcome of their teaching and research work.

'This book invites us to go on a journey, not simply of the imagination but also of activity and transformation. The invitation is to reconnect with the living forms around us by looking and doing so that our eyes are opened to the nature of plant life. The nature revealed has both the truth of scientific knowledge and the beauty of the creative act so that we experience plants as simultaneously archetypal and forever new. The door opens onto a new way of practising science as an art.'

Dr Brian Goodwin, The Open University

208pp; 270 x 210mm; colour cover; fully illustrated; ISBN 1 869 890 85 X

Tapestries
Weaving Life's Journey
Betty Staley

Tapestries gives a moving and wise guide to women's life phases. Drawing on original biographies of a wide variety of women, informed by personal experience and by her understanding of anthroposophy, Betty Staley offers a vivid account of life journeys. This book helps readers reflect on their own lives and prepare for the next step in weaving their own biographical tapestry.

336pp; 216 x 138mm; paperback; ISBN 1 869 890 15 9

Water, Electricity and Health
Protecting Yourself from Electrostress at Home and Work
Alan Hall

This book will help you understand how electrostress affects you. Symptoms can range from fatigue, tension and poor resilience to insomnia, low immunities and serious illness. New light is cast on the secrets of water, life and electricity.

When physicist Alan Hall found that underground streams linked a stricken home to nearby power cables, the family moved and recovered their health. He then asked how water transmits electrostress. Here, he invites you to accompany his fascinating journey of discovery into the nature of water as bearer of life, and as carrier of death. His major discovery of biodynamic fields is applied to countering the harmful effects of electromagnetic fields. He shows how to take steps to neutralise electrostress and increase your energy.

A must for anyone working in health, in biodynamics and new science. This book is also accessible to anyone concerned with electrostress caused by electromagnetic fields in the home or workplace.

'An intriguing book that explains in a lucid but simple style the problems of Electropollution'   *The Homeopath,* 69

192pp; 210 x 135mm; paperback; ISBN 1 869 890 94 9

Who's Bringing them Up?

Television and Child Development: How to Break the TV Habit

Martin Large

Updated with recent research, this book describes the effects of television viewing on children's play, senses, thought, imagination, social skills, learning and growth. The author argues that young children need protection from such a powerful medium. Practical ways of giving up the 'T.V. habit' are described so that readers can take positive steps to build a more creative family life.

192pp; 210 x 135mm; paperback; illustrations; ISBN 1 869 890 24 8

Orders

Ordering information from:

Hawthorn Press
1 Lansdown Lane, Stroud, Gloucestershire
GL5 1BJ. United Kingdom
Tel: (01453) 757040   Fax: (01453) 751138
E-mail: hawthornpress@hawthornpress.com

If you have difficulties ordering from a bookshop, you can order direct from:

Scottish Book Source Distribution
137 Dundee Street, Edinburgh
EH11 1BG
United Kingdom
Tel: (0131) 229 6800   Fax: (0131) 229 9070

All Hawthorn Press titles are available in North America from:

Anthroposophic Press
3390 Route 9, Hudson,
NY 12534
U.S.A.
Tel: (518) 851 2054   Fax: (518) 851 2047